Stripped

A Journey From Rejection To Redemption

Sherrell,

I pray my story is a blessing!

Mary Stewart-Holmes
127 Scott Rd.
Waterbury, CT 06705
203-539-1186
info@comebackqueen.org
www.comebackqueen.org

Published by Bodhi Alliance Press

Limits of Liability and Disclaimer of Warranty

The author and/or publisher shall have neither liability nor responsibility to anyone with respect to any loss or damage caused, or alleged to be caused, directly or indirectly by the information contained in this book.

Warning – Disclaimer

This is a work of creative nonfiction. The events are portrayed to the best of my memory. While all the stories in this book are true, some names and identifying details have been changed to protect the privacy of the people involved. In some cases I have compressed events; in others I have made two people into one. The conversations in the book all come from my recollections, though they are not written to represent word-for-word transcripts.

Stripped

A Journey From Rejection To Redemption

Mary Stewart-Holmes

To find out how to help prevent suicide,
teen pregnancy, sexual and physical abuse,
and childhood molestation go to
www.comebackqueen.org

Acknowledgments/Dedication

This book is dedicated to my sons: Kenny & "Zigga" — my biggest blessings. Also to my husband, Terry, who pushed me to open up and not hold back. I don't know if this book would be what it is without you! To my late mother and grandparents, Rosemary, Roosevelt, and Louise — I am who I am today because of all that you instilled in me. I dedicate this book to you.

Thank you, God, for guiding, protecting, and loving me unconditionally throughout this journey.

I would also like to acknowledge all those who made this book possible. Divya Parekh and Bodhi Alliance Press and their team of editors, formatters, and graphic designers; cover designer eightwonine; photographer Orville Anthony Wright and Coche Productions; and Lisa Marie Pepe and the Art of Unlearning Family.

Thank you to my sisters Keyshea and Tawana; my brothers Jermaine and Keith; the McKinney / Burton Family; and the Holmes Family for your moral support. Thank you, Simone Turner; my "Junior Editors" Alissa, Toni, Shamika, and Sam; Dr. Tiana Von Johnson; Senator Marilyn Moore; Dr. Marco Clark; and CICA International University.

Thank you to my mother-in-law, Dr. Shirley Holmes, for your encouragement and prayers. To my Triumph Church family, Martha Melvin, Suzanne Howard, Doris Brown, Torie Brow n, Kasha Edwards, Dawn Merlo, Nile Sykes — thank you all for your support along my journey!

Special thank you to Daniel, Shaniya, Jamal, Ja'Vian, Isaiah, and Sarah — Mimi loves you! To everyone who encouraged me, motivated me, and made an impact on my life, thank you! To you, the reader, thank you for allowing me to open up and bare my soul.

About the Author

Dr. Mary Stewart-Holmes is a #1 International Best Selling Author, second year law student, and award-winning non-profit founder. Mary is available for speaking engagements, mentorship, and public appearances. Mary takes an interest in assisting young women who struggle with rejection, depression, abuse, and other social-emotional issues.

For booking, contact booking@comebackqueen.org.

Table of Contents

Chapter 1

The Beginning of the End

Everyone has a story. Mine has episodes of sex, drugs, and hitting rock bottom. Oh, and self-discovery. Self-discovery is definitely in there. Before I get to that, let me tell you how a shy, introverted girl collided with molestation, rape, abuse, teen pregnancy, promiscuity, prostitution, prison, and every other vile "p" word.

I lived on the edge in ways that could have killed me. In fact, there were times when I wanted it to kill me! However, while I was too afraid to jump and end it all in an instant, I was also too scared to walk away. The addiction to the rush of being so close to living and dying at the same time was the only thing that distracted me from my broken life.

Yeah, broken describes my life. And I am *still* picking up pieces of my shattered childhood. Still discovering shards of bitterness, rejection, and self-erected strongholds lying in the most unsuspecting places.

My story has flaws and failures, but it is also full of fortitude and all types of fabulousness. It is a journey that I never thought would end well. Not everyone gets a happy ending; especially if you have seen the things I have seen and done the things I have done. Many people that know me may read this story and walk away shocked at the sordid details of my life. To those who know me, I say this: You think you know me, but you have no idea!

Initially, I thought it best to start at the beginning. However, I realized that my life has consisted of many "beginnings."

Over the years, I have found myself continually rebooting as I reel back from one trauma or another. Facing setbacks and bouncing back from them has become second nature to me. Unfortunately, some of those shocks had such a lasting effect that they trickled down into a larger body of issues that I eventually felt I would drown in without hope of ever returning to the surface. The scariest part of it all is that I can't swim.

So, let's start at the beginning of the end. The beginning starts in South Carolina on the side of a building where I was sexually molested against a concrete wall. I was just four years old.

My memories from those years are murky. What I do remember is the swing set that was in the middle of the playground, the monkey bars, and the smell of freshly cut grass and how it would stick to my sneakers as we would run and play early in the mornings.

The grass would make my skin itch, which was already bright pink by the constant scratching at the mosquito bites on my arms and legs. My cousins and I would play for hours with very little supervision — the perfect environment for mischief.

An older relative would sometimes keep an eye on us little ones, and the way he played with us made us forget that he was an adult. He would have a radiant smile and the loudest laugh when he tickled my sides. Rolling on the ground in laughter until I was out of breath, I was too full of innocent joy to push him away when he started tickling me down there.

Some things just have a way of burning themselves into your consciousness. One of those things for me was when I first felt a surge of electricity shoot through my body when this older man touched me in a way that we both knew was wrong. However, I didn't stop him because it felt good and ticklish.

It made me giggle.

In between all the giggling and squirming to break free from his large hands, I had no idea that my innocence was slowly coming undone.

One day, after all the playing, he somehow pulled me to the side of one of the white buildings. While I can't remember his exact words, I remember the look in his eyes. It was a look that told me something was not right. The smile on his face seemed to be hiding something, and it scared me.

All of a sudden, I felt as if I wanted to run away, but I knew he would catch me and I didn't want him to tickle me anymore. I just wanted to go home. He hugged me and reassured me that he wouldn't tell anyone what we were doing because he didn't want me to get into trouble. While hugging me, he picked me up and put his large jacket over me. It covered my entire body.

He put his hands in the back of my pants and began moving his fingers between my bottom and then down there. Although I was only four years old, I could sense something wasn't right.

It felt okay and wrong at the same time, and I didn't know which feeling was the right one to feel. I just buried my face in his sweaty shirt and hoped we wouldn't get caught.

If anyone had walked by it would have looked as if he was hugging a small child close to him. His jacket hid from public view the disgusting things he was doing to me — a four-year-old girl!

Was I supposed to know this was wrong and tell somebody? Or was I supposed to keep quiet and tell him to stop? I'm not sure if I even knew what was happening to me at such a young age.

One day he told me to pull my pants down and bend over because he wanted to show me something. I don't know why

I listened to him, but I did. I bent over, and he began licking me down there. He did it so fast, and it was over so quickly that when he asked me if it felt good, I just giggled because all I knew was that it tickled.

"Do you want me to do it again?" he asked.

I nodded "yes."

He quickly licked me again, and I pulled my pants up and ran away, hoping no one had seen us. The sexual abuse continued for almost a year until my mother moved my siblings and me back to Connecticut where I would continue kindergarten.

I remember feeling much older than the rest of my classmates. In fact, I thought it was normal to feel myself with my hands and other objects to get that same ticklish feeling.

What happened during that year in South Carolina remained a secret, and when my mother announced that we would be moving back down south before I could even start first grade, I felt a twinge of fear.

However, this fear was not that I would be touched again down there. Instead, it was because I started to look forward to it and that we would somehow get caught. My innocent thoughts were the beginning of self-blame. It was the start of a downward spiral of me telling myself that I had somehow asked for it and that I deserved it.

Looking back over those years, I now know that I didn't ask to be molested. He forced himself on me, and I was too young to understand that he was abusing me. I was far too young to consent, and the abuser was manipulating me by doing things that felt good to me and reminding me that if anyone ever found out, I would get into trouble.

To this day, my family is unaware of what happened to me back then. It's funny how secrets work. We hide things for many reasons: to avoid trouble, to protect others, and to defend ourselves. We hide to prevent others seeing us.

As my mother often said, "What's done in the dark always comes to light."

Chapter 2

That Man

To this day, I often wonder if anything would have been done if I had told someone about the molestation. Every time I think about it, I quickly remind myself that every known child molester in my family still comes to the family cookouts, the holiday gatherings, reunions, weddings, and funerals.

I will not apologize for the truth, but I want to warn my family to buckle up from this point forward. No one has ever gone to jail or suffered any consequences for their actions unless you count others whispering about you. That is all we ever seem to do — whisper!

I am tired of whispering. I want to talk about it. No, I want to scream about it at the top of my lungs! I want to yell until I drown out the voices in my head that blame me. The voices in my head that tell me, "You don't air your dirty laundry." Then there are the ghosts in my family tree that haunt and taunt me with words like, "Who do you think you are? You think you're special? You're not the only one that had someone molest you, so get over it!"

When I was around ten years old, I boldly asked my mom why we never call the police when we find out that a family member molested another family member. The abuse was, unfortunately, a common occurrence in our family.

"Mommy, why doesn't anyone call the cops on him?" I asked.

I was referring to an older cousin who had recently molested one of my baby cousins.

"I don't know," she responded.

"So, why don't you call the cops?" I insisted.

"If his mother doesn't want to get the police involved, then I'm not going to turn him in and have her mad at me."

Judging by the tone of her voice, I knew she was getting aggravated, and that she would soon be scolding me since I asked too many "grown-up" questions – so I let it go.

However, I desired to tell someone. I wanted to talk to someone about what was happening in my family, but every time I overheard the adults talking about it, they made sexual abuse sound normal. It was as if it was nothing more than family gossip that got discussed over cigarettes and soda.

Therefore, I remained silent.

When my mother moved us back down south, I thought she was staying with us. As she was leaving, I cried and clung to her and wished that she could wait just a little while longer before she moved. I had no idea that it would be two years before I could live with her again.

Now and then, she would come for a visit, but that wasn't good enough for me. Meanwhile, I latched onto my grandmother because she was the only other mother figure that I knew. My grandmother called me her baby, and I must admit she spoiled me. I even slept in her bed so much that my granddaddy had to get a second bed to sleep in because he "didn't feel right sleeping next to a little girl."

Their bedroom became "our" bedroom. My artwork from school covered the wall on "my side" of the bed, and my clothes and toys soon found their way into their dresser drawers. My grandparents' house protected me from the older relative that had previously molested me because there was always someone around — especially my siblings.

Excitement, play, and noise frequently filled the house. We ran around the house, through the woods, up the road, and everywhere in between. We didn't care that there were only three channels on the small television set we owned.

My innocence was back. While I missed my mom, I quickly adjusted to my new life. In many ways, life felt better in South Carolina. I was in a two-parent household, and my grandfather felt more like a father than any other male figures I had in my life at that age.

I was the only child that didn't have a father. One of my sisters had a father who we called Chucky. He would claim all of us, although we knew she was his only biological child. In my mind, I secretly wished he was my dad also. After all, we were both light-skinned with long, wavy hair. My sister's constant reminders that he was not my father repeatedly crushed my hopes. She even told me I was adopted at one point.

My mother never told me about my father, but she never had any issues telling me who my father wasn't. She would say to me that Chucky wasn't my father, and neither was the man who signed my birth certificate. She said he came into the picture after she was already pregnant with me and he wanted a child.

Sadly, he turned out to be a deadbeat dad that left before I even knew he was there. I often wondered how you voluntarily sign up for something and then bail out.

I was looking for a father figure to fill the void that existed in my life. My grandfather sort of filled that space. He wasn't very talkative, but he at least let me ride with him every day when he would pick up my grandmother from her job at the plant.

He would also let me watch him work on building things in his shed and talk his ear off about things I did in school. He was a great listener! He had a bumper sticker on the back of his car that read: "I may be slow, but at least I'm ahead of you." He had a sense of humor that very few understood, but whether you got the joke or not, you laughed out of respect.

That was the closest I would get to a father figure until *he* came along. I am not going to mention his name, so let's call him "That Man." He showed up the year our mom came back to get us. They came down together with big news. They were married!

To our surprise, Mommy wanted to marry That Man again, but this time with everyone present. We were all going to move back to Connecticut together and live happily ever after.

I had to be about eight years old when we left my grandparents' house and moved back north. I let go of the father figure I had in my granddaddy and latched on to That Man. I didn't know anything about That Man, except that my mother was in love. If she loved him, so did I.

That Man and I grew close for the first year. So close, in fact, that my siblings began to resent me for bonding with him. They directed the hatred they had for That Man towards me. They had picked up something about That Man that I was too young and innocent to see. It turns out, they were right.

For the next few years, I witnessed an almost slow-motion shattering of my family structure. My brother would continuously bounce back and forth between our home and our aunt's house after repeated fights with That Man. One day my brother never returned. That Man had a drinking problem that would fuel his fits of unprovoked anger, which began to spiral out of control. Shortly after, my mother and I started finding drugs in the house.

"Mommy, what's this?" I held up a brown medicine bottle that looked like it had a straw melted into the side of it.

Her eyes grew wide as she snatched the bottle out of my hand and quickly inspected it. "Somebody tried to make a crack pipe; that's what it is," she said.

I had no idea what she meant, but based on what I had learned in one of my D.A.R.E. classes, I knew that it had to do with drugs.

"You mean, somebody used this to smoke crack?" I asked.

"Yup. And then they had the nerve to try and hide it!"

Although she was careful not to implicate That Man, I knew he was the culprit. Not too long after this discovery, she was cleaning the top of the China cabinet and found multiple vials of cocaine lined up across the inside of the top border.

I vividly remember the red caps and the small bright tubes that were exactly like the ones I would see in the backyard of our house, on the ground on the way to college, and even in our hallway before they evicted all the drug dealers and dope addicts. I also knew what they were and what they contained because of what I had seen in my favorite movie, "New Jack City."

"Look at this," she said while holding the vials in her hand. "This don't make no sense. He wait 'til he gets home." Her southern accent was thick as molasses.

Unsure of what to say, I stood there in silence. By this time, we all knew That Man was strung out on drugs because he was selling everything in the house from our stereo system to the television sets.

He even sold my VCR tapes of "Showtime at the Apollo," "Def Comedy Jam," and "Soul Train." Someone told me they saw him on the streets trying to sell the recordings out of the trunk of his car. However, he was so high that people were just taking the tapes without paying for them.

One night, not long after Christmas, I caught him taking my new mountain bike down the stairs to sell it. He took one look at me and brought it back inside without saying a word. Guilty!

Chapter 3

Boy Crazy

My family was being destroyed! The façade of the perfect family was going up in smoke as my mother's husband continued to drive a deeper wedge between my siblings and me.

As I mentioned, they resented me for liking That Man from the beginning, but I was just a little girl longing for acceptance. When he opened his arms to me, I fell for him hook, line, and sinker.

My mother tried to stay with That Man while he battled his demons. She left a few times, but she always came back. She kicked him out a few times too, but still, he would crawl back into our lives. It was even more of a struggle to watch That Man singing in church and working as a deacon while he secretly tore our house apart with his drug addiction.

By this time, my oldest sister had left the house, leaving my second oldest sister and me to go at each other's throats. I was the baby, and we never seemed to get along. The constant fighting was the last thing my mother needed while she sorted through the remains of her marriage.

Meanwhile, as I was nearing the end of sixth grade, I tried to escape the pain of what was going on at home by turning all of my attention to boys. By this time, I was with my third boyfriend, and I considered this one to be "serious." He was someone that had his eye on me for a couple of years, but we started to officially "go out" early that school year.

Travis was the most popular and probably the cutest boy in the entire school! He was the most athletic, the tallest, the fastest, and the best dressed. Although I was flattered that he had such a crush on me, I was reluctant to date him because all the girls liked him.

Looking back on those years, I was way too young to have such adult thoughts, but hey – this is how the girls acted in "The Babysitter's Club" and "Sweet Valley High," right? Every book that I read seemed to center around some boy-crazy teen, so I did the same thing. However, I had never even kissed a boy. To keep my mind off the chaos at home, I made it my mission to have my first kiss before leaving elementary school.

But here was the big problem: I was horrified at the thought that if I kissed Travis, then he would immediately know it was my first time and my inexperience would be exposed. So, I did what most kids did back then – I practiced on my arm! After a few private sessions, I was ready, or so I thought. One day, Travis and I were hanging around in his house when he suggested playing the game Truth or Dare. I knew exactly where this was headed, but I feigned innocence and played along anyway.

It didn't take long for Travis to dare me to kiss him. So predictable, but this was the moment I had been dreading. I couldn't relax, I couldn't focus, and I didn't know what to do. He leaned in toward me. I closed my eyes. I felt myself slowly leaning toward him. It seemed like an eternity had passed with no action, so I opened my eyes. Travis was just staring at me with a half-amused/half-confused look on his face. It was then that I realized that I still had my lips squeezed together in a pucker.

Blushing, I looked away and laughed it off. "What? I was waiting for you!" I said through the laughter.

"Um, I was wondering what in the world you were doing," he said. "Have you ever even kissed before?"

Now I was even more embarrassed. "Of course. Who hasn't?"

The next day, when I walked into class, Travis and his friends were pointing at me and laughed. "Mary kisses like she's sucking on a lemon!"

The entire classroom erupted in laughter. If looks could kill, my angry stare would have shot Travis. I was furious!

"You dummy! You're the one that wanted to kiss me!" I said.

The laughter continued. I got so mad that I picked up a pair of scissors off the teacher's desk and threw it at him. The scissors stuck into the wall beneath the chalkboard.

The class became silent. It seemed like shock paralyzed Travis for a moment, but when he snapped out of it, I could tell by the look in his eyes that he was enraged. He grabbed one of the massive, metal classroom chairs and threw it at me with all his strength. I quickly dodged the chair, but it hit a kid name Ephraim, who was standing behind me, square in the stomach. Ephraim doubled over in pain, and slowly fell to the floor. At that moment, all hell broke loose in the class!

Travis ran after me, I ran into the hallway, someone yelled for the nurse, other students circled Ephraim, and others chased Travis and me down the hallway yelling and screaming. Just like that, my relationship with Travis was over. Luckily, soon after this episode my mother would leave her husband and move us to a nearby town called Stratford. It was the perfect time for all of us to start over.

Unfortunately, that was the furthest thing from the truth.

It wasn't long after the move to Stratford that That Man moved back in with us. I was devastated. I thought we had finally escaped, but somehow, he convinced her to let him back in. I drowned out the drama at home by going to parties, getting into fights, smoking weed, and jumping from one boyfriend to the next.

I was the new girl on the block with yellow skin, long hair, and a pretty face. My looks garnered lots of attention from the young boys in my neighborhood and even some of the older men, to be quite honest. Things were somewhat starting to feel like a fresh start. On the flip side, all the attention from the opposite sex caused me to make lots of enemies among the female population at my new school.

The fights and the arguments seemed to happen almost on a daily basis. I became accustomed to being taunted and jumped by multiple females. One fight in particular was incredibly unfair. The girls were older and bigger and were fighting me so hard that I felt my only chance at getting out of this fight was to pull out my box cutter.

That is just what I did!

With my head down, and Janet Jackson "Poetic Justice" braids swinging, I sliced thin air several times before I made contact with flesh. I sliced one of the girls in the face, and they quickly dispersed.

Meanwhile, someone called the cops. When they arrived, I ended up handcuffed in the back of the police car. It all happened so fast that it went by in a blur — until I realized one of the cops had my purse. My heart dropped when I saw him carefully searching through the contents.

It was one of those small, clear plastic purses that were trending big that year. My bag contained something that I did not want the cop to find. I panicked and thought to myself, "If he finds the drugs in my bag, my life is over!"

My purse contained quite a few odds and ends, including a cylinder-shaped M&M container that would typically hold bite-sized M&M's. However, I had replaced the candy with dime bags of marijuana that I planned on selling at a club called The Legion. Teen parties happened there every weekend.

I hoped that the police officer would overlook the candy container, but he flipped open the top. My heart started pounding even faster! I felt like I was suffocating and helpless because there was nothing I could do at that point.

The police officer looked at me through the window of the cop car. My heart could have stopped right then and there! He looked back into the container, closed it, and placed it back into my purse. I don't know why he spared me, but he did. To this day, I wonder what would have become of my life had I ended up with a drug charge on my record. I am so grateful to God that I never had to find out.

That cop had mercy on me. You would think this would have scared me straight and turned me off from a life of crime. Sadly, things did not end there — they only got worse.

Chapter 4

Appetite for Destruction

I continued to sell drugs and joined a pseudo-gang of young men where I was the Lil' Kim to their Junior Mafia. It was short-lived and something that we did just for fun, but it sparked something dark inside of me. Suddenly, I realized that I had a taste for danger. I rode around in stolen cars, hung out until the morning, and jumped random females just because a friend of a friend had a beef with so and so.

Danté Jones, one of my male friends, would steal cars almost every day. I took note of this because he would park the stolen rides near my house, and I could see them from my bedroom window. Because I had nothing better to do that summer, I decided that I would steal cars with him. We would go to the local mall and break the quarter glass (the smaller, triangular window) on the vehicles. After he got the car started, within what seemed like mere seconds, we would just drive off.

We rode around the neighborhood as if the cars belonged to us. Danté probably didn't even have a license to drive. In fact, one day we got so high on weed that we were sitting at a stop sign and thought it was a red light! We were waiting for the light to change and when we realized our mistake, we sat there and laughed until a cop pulled up behind us. I spotted the officer in the rearview mirror and told Danté to hurry up and drive off. He kept his foot on the brake, and just sat there laughing. Miraculously, the cop patiently waited until we slowly drove away in our stolen Lincoln Continental or whatever kind of car it was.

We lived on the edge, recklessly not caring whether we got caught or not. One cool summer night, Danté drove out to a condo complex to get a new ride because the one we had was getting too hot (meaning it was too risky to continue flaunting it through the neighborhood). While waiting for Danté to select the right car to steal, I watched him as he slipped into the shadows of the parking lot. It was a nicer part of town, and while only ten minutes from where we lived, it seemed like a whole new world. All was quiet except for the sound of crickets, and the tiny purr of an engine in the distance, which alerted me to the fact that Danté must have selected his toy for the evening.

Sure enough, within seconds he was pulling out of the lot with another Lincoln. The car came fully loaded — even had a baby car seat in the back. I looked back at the car seat with a guilty feeling in the pit of my stomach. At that moment, I realized that we were not just stealing a car, we were taking away something precious from a family. We were violating someone that could have easily been our mothers, fathers, aunts, uncles, etc. It wasn't fun anymore.

The next day, I decided to hang with a guy who had been pursuing me. I chose this impromptu date over the usual joy ride and smoke out session with Danté. Later that day, my pager kept going off "911." It was Danté. I rushed to call him back to see if he was OK.

"Yo! My car flipped!" Danté said frantically.

"Wait, what? What do you do mean, your car flipped?" I asked.

"The cops were chasing us! I had this chick in the car, and the cops chased us downtown. When I turned under the bridge, the car flipped like two or three times!"

I had never heard him sound scared before, but I could hear the fear in his voice. "She's real hurt. Head all bloody."

"Who did you have in the car? What were y'all doing?" I didn't know what else to say or ask.

"It was Janette. You know, the chick from the barbecue? She's at the hospital now. I don't even know if she's all right," he said.

"Are you OK? Are you hurt?" I asked.

He responded, "Yeah, my arm is bruised up and my ankle feels twisted, but other than that I'm cool."

It turns out that he had to pull her from the wrecked car, bruised and bloody. He also had to get her to the hospital all while trying to avoid being captured by the police. It could have easily been me. You would think that this would have served as another wake-up call, but my taste for danger did not dissipate. While my joyriding days were over, I would soon pick up another vice.

One of my high school friends would steal clothes from the mall and other local stores, but I never wanted to participate because my philosophy was that if I took what didn't belong to me, I would eventually lose more than what I had stolen. Oh, I was not the epitome of a law-abiding citizen, nor was I a "goody two shoes" by any stretch of the imagination, but I had boundaries. I naturally found it difficult to steal. Cars, yes. Clothes, no. I know, my morals were all out of whack. I had already given up stealing cars. Stealing halter tops and capri pants were not worth going to jail over, in my opinion. Then one day, I realized just how easy it was to take six items into a fitting room and come out with five.

I wish that I could go back in time and tell my younger self that it is so not worth it. When you are getting what you want, when you want it, regardless of how much money is in your pocket, you become egotistical, materialistic, and downright greedy. I came up with what I thought was an airtight plan. I would only take what I could wear under my clothes. After getting caught a few times and being allowed to leave with a simple warning to stay out of the store, I became cocky and arrogant.

I started getting bolder, and would sometimes walk right out of the store with a brand-new purse on my arm that was a completely different style and color than the one I had when I came into the store. I would wear jeans under my jeans, jackets underneath my coats, wear jewelry out of a store, and even put brand new shoes on my feet — leaving my own worn, unwanted flats or sandals behind in the shoebox that I would nonchalantly place back on the store rack.

One Christmas season, I started boosting for co-workers. There was no shame in my game. I would walk into the store with one of the store's bags hidden in my jacket, and leave with that bag filled with items as if I had purchased it. One of the stores I liked to target did not use sensors that would buzz if the sales associate neglected to remove it at the cash register. Naturally, I frequented that store and would rack up items from there on a weekly basis.

One day, while stuffing my shopping bag with clothing, I realized that they started using these new stickers the store strategically placed on the inside fold of an expensive jacket. At first glance, it appeared to be nothing to worry about, but when I peeled it back, there was a metal pattern underneath that would have gotten me caught. I hurriedly peeled off all the stickers and stuck them in a pocket of a pair of jeans and moved on.

I suppose they eventually caught on that the sticker sensors were not working. They upgraded to sensors that were plastic on one end with a little metal cap on the other. These were easy to pop off with a pair of pliers, so with a small tool on hand, and a quick scoping out of the store's blind spots, I again began to rack up hundreds of dollars' worth of items every week. I thought I was in the clear, but apparently, they decided that the sticker sensors were worth another shot.

I became so comfortable and secure in my ability to remove the plastic sensors that I did not realize that they had reverted to the stickers. One item had the sticker still on it when I walked past the exit doors. Of course, the security officer stopped me and asked me for my receipt. When I tried to run off, another associate grabbed me, and they detained me. Fortunately, they let me go. Unfortunately, this would not deter me from stealing again.

It would take years before I overcame my appetite for destruction. I recall saying to myself as a teenager, "Everything you touch, you destroy. You just have a bad habit of making a mess of your life." The first time I spoke these discouraging words to myself was when I was fourteen years old and pregnant.

Chapter 5

Fourteen and Pregnant

My boyfriend, Juan, and I were inseparable. No one could convince us that we weren't going to be together forever. We had so much sex that we started a contest with another couple in high school about how many unusual places we could find to have sex. We had sex behind the vending machine near the school gym, in the girls locker room, and in the middle of the chorus room where the choir sang songs like "Swing Low, Sweet Chariot." We did it under the trampoline in his backyard (the mosquito bites were brutal). We were in his pool, his mom's bed, and on his front porch. We had sex in the Dunkin' Donuts bathroom, in the library, and in the cemetery behind the library. You get the point. We won that bet.

Now you see how I ended up pregnant at fourteen. The interesting thing about all of this: I would not experience an orgasm until years later in my early twenties. I had no idea that I was supposed to climax as well! Once I discovered the big "O," I looked back on those childhood romps and thought, "Boy, was I dumb." I can't be too hard on myself though. I was engaging in an activity I wasn't yet woman enough to handle.

Juan and I convinced ourselves that we would be together until we were old and gray, watching our grandchildren run circles around our rocking chairs. So, when my belly started to protrude indicating that I was definitely carrying his child, we were excited and started making plans for our future together. We knew our parents wouldn't like it, but we planned to make sure they knew we were up to the task of caring for the baby ourselves.

What scared me most was breaking the news to my mother. I knew it would crush her because she only wanted the best for me. It was not in her plans to see me barely entering into my teenaged years with a baby on the way. My best bet was to wait until I was too far along for her to force me to have an abortion.

One day, my mother took me for my routine dental checkup, and all was going well until the dental assistant asked me if I was pregnant. I was shocked by the question and did not realize it was standard procedure to ask female patients if they are pregnant before conducting an x-ray. I didn't know what to say, so I just stared at the assistant with what I am sure was a very telling look on my face.

"Listen, honey," she said, "don't worry. Everything you tell me is confidential. Are you pregnant right now?"

"Yes," I said. I could barely muster the word.

"Do your parents know?"

I shook my head "no."

"You do know that you will have to tell them eventually, right?"

"If I tell my mother, she's going to give me a whooping," I confessed. "I might lose the baby if I get in trouble."

By this time, I was shedding full-blown tears. I had a very real fear that my mother would beat my baby out of me. She was a soft-spoken woman when she wanted to be, but my mother had some strict ways and a heavy belt that put the fear of God in all of us.

"We have social workers here that can help you tell your parents," she said. "I'll take you to speak with them and come up with a plan on how to break the news."

She was so reassuring that I agreed to let one of the social workers come to the house to meet with my mom and me so that I could tell her that I was carrying her grandchild. When the social worker walked into our house, I could tell my mother already knew what was going on.

"You done got yourself pregnant, didn't you?" my mother asked in her southern accent. She had a way of cutting you without a knife. I just started crying. There was nothing I could say or do at this point but surrender.

I nodded my head "yes" in between the sobbing.

"You just had to be grown," she continued. "Now you gonna find out what it means to be grown. I'm gonna take your butt down to that clinic and get you an abortion."

I started weeping even louder and pleading for her to let me have my baby. I told her that Juan and I were prepared to take care of the baby on our own. After all, he had a job at a Subway sandwich shop, and his oldest sister agreed to help us with babysitting during school hours. But, there was no convincing her – her mind was made up.

She made an appointment at a local abortion clinic after speaking with Juan's mother. They agreed to split the cost and punished us by refusing to let us see each other after school. However, when the day arrived for me to have the surgical procedure, Juan snuck out and met me at the clinic. When we saw each other, he grabbed me and held me close to him, and we cried and told each other how much we wanted our baby.

"You don't have to do this," Juan said. "I found out that if you tell them you don't want to do it, they can't go through with it. Tell them you don't want it."

Sure enough, they held a counseling session before the procedure, and when they asked me if I wanted an abortion, I told them "no."

A few minutes later, one of the nurses escorted me out to the lobby where my mom was waiting. When they told her that I refused the abortion, she went into a rage.

"What did I tell you?" she said. "You want to wait until you are so far along that they won't be able to put you to sleep when they cut that baby out of you?"

I don't know if that was true or not, but it scared me enough to comply. Juan and I were devastated that we could not keep our child. What put the final nail in the coffin of our relationship was when my mother tried to press charges against Juan for statutory rape because he was sixteen-years-old. Thankfully, she did not succeed in having him arrested, but the damage was done. We broke up a few months later.

We entered a new year in high school, and it seemed as if everyone knew about our summer shenanigans with the pregnancy and abortion. Suddenly, Juan's popularity skyrocketed, and girls showered him with attention. The stress of our parents trying to keep us apart and my constant emotional breakdowns took a toll on our relationship. Not surprisingly, he eventually cheated with several girls and even brought one of them to his house to meet his family. As a young, inexperienced girl, I blamed myself.

I even got to the point where I felt so worthless and useless that I made my first suicide attempt. I locked myself in the bathroom at Juan's house and swallowed a bunch of lethal-looking pills. It turns out it was just his acne medication, but at the time I thought I could do some serious damage. The only thing that ended up happening was a major embarrassment and some yucky black tar that I had to drink to absorb the medicine in my system.

Epic fail.

When I look back over my life, I am grateful that I did not succeed. There was so much more to life than a teenage love, and sex with a horny sixteen-year-old with acne. Admittedly, I was head over heels in love at the time, but in hindsight, I admit that he was not worth dying for.

It was a crucial time in my life when I fell in love with Juan. I had experienced some trauma in my life (more details on that later), and it was vital that I had someone who could give me an escape from all the madness going on in my house.

After attempting suicide, I was ordered to talk to a psychologist. Dr. Crawford was a kind man, with a soft, gentle voice who helped me talk about my feelings in a safe environment. I was embarrassed to be seeing a psychologist because, in my mind, therapy was for "crazy" people. I very much needed it at the time, and I enjoyed my after-school sessions with him. The therapy helped me to cope with what was going on in my life back then, but my new positive outlook on therapy all came to a screeching halt after an incident with Juan's best friend, Jimmy.

Jimmy was a prankster and a jokester, and we always went at each other like the television characters Martin and Pam. To be honest, Jimmy secretly had a crush on me, but one of our "fights" turned serious after I broke up with Juan. We were walking in the hallway at school when Jimmy taunted me about my insecurities and my flat chest. He was relentless with his insults and kept hurling them at me until I reached my breaking point. Wham! I slapped him across his face. Before I could brace myself, he pushed me across the hall.

I hit the concrete wall, but I came back at him with a vengeance, ready to fight. We fought it out until Mrs. Lebovitz came out of her classroom and broke it up. We were both suspended that day, and Jimmy almost got kicked off the basketball team. He could remain on the team if he complied with one stipulation: attend a joint counseling session with yours truly.

So, there we were — forced to attend therapy together. To my dismay, the psychologist listed on our referrals was none other than my therapist, Dr. Crawford. I panicked. The last thing I wanted was for Jimmy to find out that I was seeing a therapist. I just knew he would tell everyone at school. Nevertheless, I had to go.

Dr. Crawford assured me that no one would ever know that we had spoken previously, and not long after we entered into the group therapy session, Jimmy and I found common ground and made progress. We decided to squash our differences and remain cordial despite my horrible breakup with his friend.

After returning to school from suspension, I encountered Jimmy in the hallway. All was well, and we even playfully teased each other. Rosa, one of the school's security guards, took note of our interaction with a cautious eye. Once she realized that Jimmy and I were on good terms, she backed off. The school dismissed, and as I made my way to the stairwell to exit the building, Rosa stopped me and said, "Didn't you and Jimmy just get suspended for fighting?"

"Yes," I replied.

"Something is seriously wrong with you," she said. "You're crazy." And with that, she turned her back to me and faced the window, where she could keep a close eye on the comings and goings of the students in the parking lot.

It was not so much what Rosa said, but how she said it. The pity in her eyes, the tone of her voice, and her body language all sneered, "I feel sorry for you." As a fragile teenager who had just recovered from a suicide attempt, those words broke my spirit. I was having a hard time convincing myself that nothing was wrong with me and that I was not crazy. Now, here was an adult confirming the most damaging thought I had concerning my mental state.

I left school that day crushed. I resented her for shining a mirror on my insecurities. I did not realize how deeply her words had affected me until I saw her years later. I came back to my old high school to pick up my niece who was nearing the end of her senior year. I had to be in my late twenties. When I walked into the school, one of the first people I saw patrolling the hallways was none other than Rosa.

Years had passed since that traumatizing conversation in the stairwell. I looked at her and wondered if she remembered those words she spoke over my life. Probably not. It may seem like a small thing to some, but seeing her was like having an old wound reopened. Surprisingly, it hurt. The interesting thing about seeing Rosa was that I took note of her countenance. She looked disheveled, aged, and unhappy. I imagined that she was disgruntled about her job and had encountered traumas over the years.

There she was, carrying that same walkie-talkie, probably making twelve dollars an hour, and looking unattractive and angry. While the thought of this gave me some sense of satisfaction, what would have satisfied me would have been to take that handheld radio and break her nose with it. I am so happy that I did not act on my emotions. She was so not worth it.

Chapter 6

31 Flavors of Rejection

After Juan and I broke up, I dated a few guys, but nothing seemed to last. I got a job at a Baskin-Robbins in the mall and did pretty well for myself that summer. After about a month, I got a raise from $4.75 an hour to $5.10 an hour. I made just enough to buy clothes, weed, and blunts. My boss, Belinda, was a plus-sized woman who was married to a proud Native American man who probably weighed about a hundred pounds soaking wet.

Belinda and her husband would come in with their two children once a week to check on the store. Each time they came in, her son would snatch one of the spoons out of the customer container, dip it into the ice cream of his choice, sloppily lick the ice cream off the spoon, and double dip it back into the bucket. Ugh. Belinda wouldn't say a word, and because we were all afraid of her, we pretended he wasn't a disgusting little brat. We just made sure we didn't eat out of the same bucket.

All things considered, it was a fun place to work. In fact, one of the major perks of the job was that while on the clock we could eat whatever we wanted for free. I'm surprised I was still a size 00 when the store finally closed down. Before we pulled down the gates of the shop for the last time, I made quite a few memories in that place that I will never forget.

After being promoted to assistant manager of the store, I would open and close the shop. I even got pretty good at decorating cakes. I felt a strong sense of accomplishment for the first time in my life. Our store's location was near one of the exits of the mall, which meant I often got a chance to talk to many of the other mall employees as they were leaving after their shifts. One of the mall employees was a man named George, who was probably five to seven years my senior. He was too old to be interested in a teenager, and while he was undoubtedly attracted to me, he never crossed the line. He would watch me from a distance and give me advice on whatever situation I was dealing with at the moment. He noted one night that two men had stopped by my counter. One was a mall employee, and the other was the employee's friend.

The friend's name was Terrence, and he was "mesmerized by my beauty," as he so flirtatiously told me during that first encounter. He wanted to take me out after work. He was nineteen and I was fifteen, but that did not stop him. George took note of the interaction and felt the need to warn me about Terrence.

"Be careful," said George. "It's just something about this guy. He seems sneaky."

"What is it? He just finished high school last year, he drives two cars, and he has a decent job," I replied.

"Just be careful," he repeated.

Terrence took me to the movies, and we had a great time. He brought me home that night, and I fell asleep on his mom's couch. I intended to avoid sleeping with him on the first date, and I kept my guard up until I nodded off and fell into a deep sleep. When I woke up, Terrence was kneeling down on the side of the couch, inches away from my face, and staring at me. I thought to myself, *I barely even know this guy. What in the world is he doing?* I didn't know what to say, but I managed to ask him what was wrong. He just stared at me for a few seconds, and then he spoke words that became burned into my memory.

"You're just so beautiful," he said, with tears in his eyes. "It's weird, but I honestly feel like I am falling in love with you."

With that last line, tears just started flowing down his face. I don't believe that I would have fallen for what he was saying if the tears had not followed his words. I too began to cry. I wanted to be loved so badly. All I wanted was for someone to need me, to want me, and of course, to love me. Before I knew it, I heard myself saying, "Please, don't hurt me. Just don't hurt me."

He slipped his hands into my jeans and kissed me slowly at first, and then more aggressively. I felt my body yearning for him, so I allowed his fingers to slip inside my panties, searching desperately for what he was after all along. At that moment, I was gone because Terrence had already gotten into my head. I surrendered to the feeling of wanting to be loved and desired, so I threw caution to the wind and gave in.

With a few tugs, Terrence pulled my jeans down until my slender, fifteen-year-old hips were exposed. He paused to look at me before pulling down my panties. I will never forget the sadness in his eyes. In hindsight, it was probably guilt that I saw. He knew the game he was running. Unfortunately, I fell for it all. Brace yourself, because this story is about to get ugly.

At the beginning of our relationship, Terrence was great. For the first few weeks, he would pick me up from school, and drop me off at work. He would pick me up from work, and take me out to eat. We spent every day together it seemed, and we grew closer by the minute.

One day, it dawned on me that there were a few things about Terrence that should have raised red flags from the beginning. First, I should have been concerned about the fact that he had me sit in the backseat whenever his friends were in the car. Second, he and his friends would always joke about the way I dressed. It would go from friendly banter to downright mean, stinging insults. Lastly, whenever my best friend would come around, he would give her compliments in front of me, and make comments about the size of her butt.

Mind you, I knew I was flat chested and had the figure of an eight-year-old boy, but I didn't need him to remind me of it. With all of these signs, I realized I should have heeded the warnings of George, my faithful friend from the mall. However, I felt the need to stick things out with Terrence because I had given up my goods, and I didn't want to move on without getting my end of the bargain — true love.

He promised to love me, and I wanted him to make good on that promise! What I failed to realize, though, was that he was trying to push me away so that I could do his dirty work for him and end the relationship. I was looking to get what I wanted, but I had already given Terrence what he was after. Now that he had gotten it, he was becoming impatient with the fact that I had yet to move on so that he could conquer the next chick. Flashbacks of that night at his mom's house would come back to me; the night he cried and told me he was falling for me. It must have been one sick joke; probably something he pulled on all the girls.

A few tears, a few endearing words, and just like that, chicks fall for it every time. Or maybe it was just me. Either way, things were starting to come into full focus. Plus, there was something about Terrence that was downright scary. The way he would yell at me and disrespect me was traumatizing to my young mind. In fact, one day I called him from a payphone after a basketball game to let him know that I was on my way to his house, and he cussed me out so badly that I lost control of my bladder and peed on myself. It was not just a trickle, but a complete loss of control.

I walked twenty minutes to his house with my jeans soaked with urine. When I arrived, he and his friends just laughed at me. He gave me a pair of his jeans to wear home. When he pulled up in front of my house to drop me off, I conjured up the courage to tell him that I did not appreciate how he was treating me. I even protested about having to sit in the back seat while his friend sat up front with him. He turned around in his seat and gave me a look of pure evil that I'll never forget.

With fire in his eyes, he yelled, "Get the fuck out!"

I had never seen him this angry before. His friend even seemed to be caught off guard. I froze. I couldn't move. Finally, I started to respond but before I could even get the words out of my mouth he yelled even louder, "I said, get the fuck out!"

I rushed out of the car and slammed the door behind me. I hadn't even made it to my door before he was out of the driveway and turning the corner. As I tried to get my keys out of my purse to unlock the front door, I realized how badly my hands were shaking. I alternated wiping tears from my eyes and holding onto my belongings all while trying to rush inside the house so I could scream into my pillow.

You would think that the relationship would have ended there, but I was determined to find out why he was treating me like this. I called his mom's house phone about twenty times the next day. He never answered. He never called back. A few days later, he finally answered the phone only to coldly ask me why I was even bothering to call. It got to the point where I would get anxiety and had a strong urge to pee every time I heard the phone ring, because I was hoping it would be him returning my phone calls. Even all these years later, I still have a conditioned response to pee when the telephone rings or when I hear a voicemail recording.

Chapter 7

Slowly Dying

One day, something in me broke. I was utterly crushed, heartbroken, and emotionally exhausted. I wanted the pain to go away. The tears just wouldn't stop, but I felt like there was no end in sight to this hurt. The overwhelming desire to end it all kept returning because at least I would put an end to inviting pain into my life. My mind was made up.

I was working the cash register at my job when I decided that I would take my lunch. After cashing my check and purchasing about five large bags filled with toys, I donated everything to a Toys for Tots drive that was set up in the middle of the mall. While this gave me a small sliver of peace, I still wanted to end my life. I made my way to the drugstore and purchased a bottle of pain pills. When I got back to work, I rushed to the bathroom without saying a word to my co-workers. I didn't want them to see the tears that started to well up in my eyes.

As soon as I closed the bathroom door, I swallowed a bunch of pain pills without hesitation. I feared that if I didn't do it quickly, I would somehow talk myself out of it. After taking a few gulps of water and nearly finishing the bottle, I felt slightly sick to my stomach but nothing more. I was disappointed that I was still conscious, so I kept trying to relax so that I could eventually drift into a deep sleep. I'm not sure how much time had passed, but when one of my co-workers knocked on the bathroom door to see if I was all right, she became alarmed when I refused to come out.

Eventually, I must have said something that alerted her that something was wrong, because she told me she was calling an ambulance. When the paramedics arrived, they convinced me to come out. They told me that if I did not come with them to the hospital, I could end up living with a lifetime of physical pain instead of dying a quick death. The thought of messing up my organs and slowly dying scared me enough to open the door.

I was being brought out of the back of the store on a stretcher just as George was showing up to purchase his usual Mocha Blast. As the paramedics rolled me outside, I caught a glimpse of George looking scared, worried, and confused all at the same time. When we made eye contact, tears started flowing down my face as they pulled me out of doors and into the back of the ambulance. Someone at the hospital contacted my family, and one of my sisters was waiting for me when I got there. She witnessed them forcing me to drink a gulp of water to open my airway so they could shove a thick plastic tube down my nose and into my stomach.

It was the most painful thing I had ever experienced. My sister, who was usually tough as nails, had to look away because of all the blood that started to spurt from my nose and mouth as they struggled to pump my stomach. It was a traumatic experience that will stay with me for the rest of my life.

Hours later, I woke up to what seemed like an empty, cold hospital room. To my surprise, George, of all people, was sitting at my bedside with a cute little stuffed animal. He never asked me what happened or why. I wasn't in the mood to talk, because it was just too painful. My throat was swollen and felt like it was on fire, so I couldn't talk if I wanted to. George and I sat there in silence as he held my hand and wiped the silent tears from my face over and over.

That was the last time I saw George. When I eventually returned to work, I noticed that he never came back to the counter to order another Mocha Blast. He never stopped by to say "hello" or even to see how I was doing. I always wondered if it was just too much for him to handle. However, I'll never forget his gesture of kindness and concern. His actions let me know that the world still contained genuine people. All men were not the same. Not all men were just looking for sex. There were men out there who didn't just enter your life to take whatever they could get and move on. Some people do care. To this day, I wonder where he is and what his life is like. However, George's abandonment was all too familiar — regardless of his reasons.

Terrence never knew I attempted suicide. Even if he did know, I don't think he would have cared. One day, he just showed up at my job as if we could pick up where we left off. He came to tell me that he was sorry and that he loved me and had some great news.

"Can we spend some time together on your lunch?" he asked. "I just want to talk to you."

I thought I was over him, but instead of telling him to leave me alone, I allowed him to stay. "Where have you been all this time?" I asked. "I called, and you never called back. Why did you do that to me?"

To my surprise, his eyes lit up with excitement, and he had a huge, silly smile on his face. "The reason I haven't been able to talk is that I had to make some serious decisions," he said. "Mary, I really need to get my shit together, and I want to spend the rest of my life with you."

"Wait...what? What happened?" Terrence never ceased

to amaze me, probably not in the best way. I was just curious to know what he had up his sleeve.

"I joined the Marine Corps, and I leave for boot camp tomorrow."

I couldn't believe what I was hearing. Here I think this man was about to propose to me out of the clear blue sky, but instead, he tells me he is leaving for boot camp! In South Carolina at that! Not only leaving but going the next day! My emotions were all over the place. How dare he even come back with this crap. I thought I was over him, but it was clear that I had not gotten the closure I so desperately needed.

He said, "I just wanted to make sure you had the address of where I am going to be. Your letters are what will help me get through this."

"So you want *me* to help *you* get through this? Dude, you have a lot of nerve!" (That's what I wanted to say, but the words never actually made it out of my head).

"I know I screwed up, but I can't do this without you," he said. "I've been talking to my uncle about this, and I promise you I will be a better man."

Promise? Tuh!

"I haven't been treating you right, but I promise to make it up to you."

There was that word again. This poor excuse for a man thought it was that easy?

Sadly, it was. I would love to say that I told him to go kick rocks. However, I accepted his apology with the intent to write him now and then but to take advantage of the opportunity to move on while he was away. I never told him about the suicide attempt, because deep down inside I knew he wouldn't even care. Nevertheless, regardless of whether or not he had changed or even had the potential to change, I decided that I would pick up what was left of my self-esteem and focus on myself. In fact, by that time I had already started seeing someone else. They say that the quickest way to get over your ex is to move on to your next.

So much for focusing on myself, right?

The first problem was that I was still a child. At this young stage in my life, I was already developing a horrible habit of associating my worth with how many men I could attract. The second problem was that I was attracting flies and fleas with my honey. My innocence and inexperience in life, combined with my rebellious nature, was attracting predators and pedophiles. While Terrence had just turned twenty years old, my new flame was in his late thirties when he started pursuing me.

Chapter 8

Always Follow the Red Card

My new flame was an older man named Jonathan. While I knew he was much older, I allowed myself to assume he was in his late twenties instead of late thirties. He never corrected me on this assumption, and he would just laugh and comment on how "collegiate" I was. He would always use that term to describe me.

Collegiate. Now when I say that word, I mean it in a way that most people would say the word "manure." Back then I took it as a compliment. Now I know better. It was merely a clever ploy to convince me that I was old enough to handle someone of his age.

He would regularly comment on how smart I was, and how I had the brain of a forty-year-old woman. In hindsight, I see that he was prepping me, and shaping my perception of why an older man would be interested in dating a teenager. Thus, the manipulation began.

In less than a year, I jumped out of the proverbial frying pan and into the fire, when it came to my bitter breakup with Terrence and the manipulation of an extreme May-December relationship with Jonathan. I went from a lying cheater to an old, lying cheater. As a fifteen-year-old, I was no match for the schemes of a thirty-six-year-old man.

During the end of my sophomore year, he was picking me up from school and buying me everything I wanted. I was getting my hair done every week, brand new shoes whenever

I wanted, and a ring on almost every finger.

"I'm going to show you the world," he would say. "Gonna have these cats out here wondering how I bagged such a fly cutie, and how you bagged an OG like me."

It always felt like I was talking to a washed-up old rapper, but I went along with the flow because it was a welcomed distraction from my home situation. He took me out for dinner and a movie nearly every weekend, and I finally felt like I was living a happy life. I thought I was cautious by keeping my options open to the possibility of playing the field. However, the weekday pickups and the weekend dates were counterproductive because it kept me right by his side at every free moment.

I didn't realize that he was just controlling me by knowing my every move. In fact, when he would pick me up from school I would go work with him — and by work, I mean hustle.

Since a young kid, Jonathan hustled in almost every state up and down the East Coast. On a good week, he could make fifteen hundred dollars or more. The average person might immediately think he had to be involved in drug activity. However, his hustle involved three cards, three caps, and a tiny red ball. The three cards were for a game most people call Three Card Monte or Three Card Molly. The three caps and red ball were for what's become known as the shell game.

The game involved Jonathan shuffling three cards or moving three caps around on top of a newspaper while people bet money (or some valuable item) to guess where either the red card or the red ball was. When they lost, which usually was the case, they would end up in this cycle of trying to win their money back. Many people would lose hundreds of dollars before giving up.

Jonathan was a magician when it came to persuading people to play. He had the gift of gab and would flirt with the ladies.

"Come on, dark and lovely," he would say to an unsuspecting victim. "I see you sneaking and peaking. Take these forty dollars and buy yourself something nice on me."

Of course, when the woman would reach for the two twenty dollar bills he would go in for the kill.

"Which one do you think it is?" he said, pulling back the newspaper with the cards lying on top. "Put up twenty, and you can take these forty dollars."

"Scared money don't make money, sweetheart. I can tell you got a lot of heart with your cute self. I understand you don't want to take the chance."

At this point, he would signal me to step in and bet twenty dollars in an attempt to win.

"What about you, Miss?" he said, pointing at me. "Twenty will get you forty."

I placed the bet, won the money, and the crowd went crazy! Jonathan faked a surprised look with his mouth wide open.

"That was your money! You could have won," he said to the woman now shaking her head in regret.

Playing along, I looked at her and recited a line that worked almost every time. "Why didn't you bet? Get him the next time and walk away!"

Before he could finish shuffling the cards, the woman had her twenty dollars out ready to bet on the next round. She ended up losing one hundred sixty dollars before finally giving up.

When it came to the guys, he always appealed to the thug or the hustler by rapping or flaunting his flashy jewelry. He was a veteran at this hustle. In fact, when I was around five years old, my mother even lost money to him. I remember her telling me that the people who had won money playing the game were usually with the con artist. How ironic that I ended up playing that very same role called "stick lady." A "stick lady" or "stick man" is someone who works for the hustler, and their primary function is to bet and win. They also serve the purpose of convincing others to place bets.

Jonathan would pay me so well that I considered quitting my new job as a cashier at Dunkin' Donuts. When I finished my shift, I would immediately hop on the city bus and help him hustle people out of their hard-earned money. Hustling was a fast life, and my mind was no longer on all the negative things going on at home. I had a reason to get up in the morning and a full day of school and hustling to look forward to.

In fact, I was so wrapped up in Jonathan and making cash every day that I ignored the nice, respectable young man I worked with who was adamant about dating me. Enrique was such a gentleman, and his demeanor was always thoughtful and romantic. However, in comparison to Jonathan, he was boring and lame. He rode his bike to work sometimes and was still early for his shift. He had a beautiful voice, and one day he serenaded me with a Jon B. song. The way he sang to me gave me an indescribable feeling. I felt beautiful. It scared me.

On the one hand, I wanted to give him a shot, but on the other hand, I was well into this dating thing with Jonathan. Jonathan could give me everything I wanted (or so I thought), while Enrique did not even own a car. I had grown too materialistic for my good. One day, Enrique surprised me by accompanying me on the city bus after my shift. However, I was supposed to meet Jonathan on that same bus to hustle. Keep in mind that my job was to win and convince others to bet. So, at this point, I think this is a recipe for disaster.

Sure enough, Jonathan pulls out his makeshift board (newspaper) and proceeds to play the shell game. No one takes the bait immediately, and the time comes for me to place my bet. Enrique sees what I am about to do and tries his best to stop me. "No! It's a scam! People never win this game," he pleads. "Please, don't do it!"

The dilemma! I hesitated a moment too long, and Jonathan almost broke our cover.

"What's wrong with you?" Jonathan said. "Take the forty dollars!"

I had no choice but to place my twenty-dollar bet in an attempt to win this round.

"Come on! Twenty will get you sixty," yells Jonathan impatiently.

Enrique looked at me with a pleading look on his face. I could tell he was looking out for my best interest.

I placed the bet. I won, of course, and as Jonathan passed me my sixty dollars, Enrique looked on in disbelief. He was amazed that someone could actually win this game. Jonathan saw his reaction and immediately recognized that Enrique would be an easy target. He leaned in toward Enrique and me and begged for an opportunity to get the money back that he lost. "This time, sixty will get you one hundred!"

The bus passengers around us went wild and egged me on to bet again. They were practically doing my job for me, because now Enrique was tempted to bet as well. However, this time around I was supposed to lose on purpose. By losing, this left only two bottle caps on the board, supposedly tilting the odds in favor of whoever wants to take advantage and bet at this point. I followed through on my job and selected the bottle cap that did not have the red ball, in spite of everyone urging me to pick the obvious choice.

I lost my sixty dollars, and Enrique was determined to defend my honor. It did not take Jonathan long to persuade Enrique to place his bet.

"Now, before you do this, realize you have a fifty-fifty chance," said Jonathan. "So, I have to raise the bet. I have to. One hundred will get you *two hundred*!"

The crowd went crazy again, pushing Enrique to take the money and run. Enrique looked at me for my vote of confidence. Jonathan looked at me, expecting me to push him to bet. It took everything for me to not intervene in this train wreck that was about to take place.

Before I could say anything, Enrique handed over his money and flipped over the cap. Empty. I knew what was coming, but it caught Enrique entirely off guard. With his mouth wide open in disbelief, his facial expression read, "How could this happen?!"

I'll never forget how he sank back into his seat, crushed and defeated. He lost about half his paycheck that day. Enrique sat in silence for the rest of the bus ride. By the time we reached the mall, I knew he was expecting me to remain with him. However, I had to get back on the bus and help Jonathan catch more "vics" (a person who lost money to our hustle) on the ride back. Somehow, I had to get back on that bus without Enrique seeing me and figuring out that I was working with the hustler the entire time.

I quickly came up with an excuse that I left something on the bus and had to run back and retrieve it. I chased the bus down, relieved that Enrique had not followed me. However, as the bus pulled away, I could see that Enrique never went inside the mall. Instead, he was just standing there, waiting and watching as the bus went on its way. I decided that I would explain to Enrique that I went back on the bus in an unsuccessful attempt to get his money back.

However, when Enrique got back onto the bus a couple of hours later, he saw me do the same thing that I had done earlier. Place a bet. Win. Lose. Urge others to bet. Enrique just watched in silence, piecing it all together.

When we reached his stop, he didn't even look back at me to say goodbye. Even at work, Enrique never spoke to me again. A few days later, I quit that job at Dunkin' Donuts and began hustling with Jonathan full time.

Chapter 9

Fishscale

Every day after school I would get on the bus and work for sixty dollars a day, plus extra on the weekends. I had more money than I was making at any job at the time, and I thought I had everything I could ever want. By the time I turned sixteen, Jonathan and I were pretty serious. When my mother decided she needed to meet the guy who was keeping me out of the house so much, Jonathan panicked.

He knew that my mother would take one look at him and figure out that he was much too old to be dating her young, teenage daughter. So, he devised a plan.

"I'm going to have to slide Tyron a couple of dollars to meet your mom," Jonathan said.

"Huh?" I was utterly lost for the moment.

"I said I might have to pay Tyron to pretend to be me so that we can get your mom off my back."

Sure enough, the following night Jonathan paid Tyron to bring me home, and when my mother came to the door to meet him for the first time, Tyron was already in character. Of course, he was on his most respectful behavior when he introduced himself as Jonathan. My mother had no reason to believe that anything was amiss, and she approved of the relationship. From that day forward, whenever my mom saw Jonathan's truck pull up to the house, she never questioned who I was with.

However, back at school word had gotten out to many of my high school classmates that I was the girlfriend of the "Hustler." When people would lose money to Jonathan on the bus, they would take their frustration and anger out on me. One day while we were playing the shell game on the bus, a victim who had lost his money playing the game became extremely upset. He was ready to fight until Jonathan made it clear that he was carrying a gun.

"Get the burner, Tommy," said Jonathan, referring to the gun his friend Tommy was carrying under his jacket.

While Tommy was reaching for the gun, the disgruntled young man decided it was time for him to exit the bus. Shaken up, I got off at the next stop and started walking toward the bus stop going in the opposite direction. Wrong move. From a distance, I saw the guy from the bus walking towards me. I played it cool. As he approached, I thought to myself, *There is no way that he is going to come after me for his money.*

Unfortunately, I was dead wrong, because as he walked past me, he turned around and grabbed me by the arm. "You were with that dude on the bus," he sneered.

I gave him a puzzled look that I hoped would throw him off. "Huh?" I replied.

"Give me my money!"

"I don't have any money." I started shaking, hoping he could not see my fear.

"Yo, give me your money right now before I cap you."

He pulled out a gun from under his jacket, held it close to his side, and pointed it at me. I felt like the wind got knocked out of me. My heart was racing, and sweat soaked my shaking hands.

Unfortunately, this was the second time I'd had a gun pointed at me. The first time was at school when a classmate had convinced me to meet him under the stairwell to "talk."

We started kissing, and when I refused to go further, he pulled out a gun and pointed it at my side. He proceeded to put his hand down the front of my jeans and forced his fingers inside me. This traumatic memory raced through my mind as I stood there. I was scared then, and I was even more scared now.

The stranger was still pointing his gun at me, but he stopped asking questions and quickly began to search my pockets. After checking my jacket, he went into my jean pockets until he found a single twenty-dollar bill. He smirked, put the money in his pocket, and walked off. It was over in a flash, but I felt so violated and helpless.

When the bus came back around, I told Jonathan everything that had happened. His response to me was that I should have never gotten off the bus in the first place. He told me that my lesson learned was that if a vic got off the bus early, we should stay on until we got back to a crowded location. It was the first time I felt that his money meant more than anything else — including me. It was all about the hustle.

That summer we made so much money that Jonathan and I had to take garbage bags filled with cash to his Uncle Vincent's house out in the suburbs. Jonathan did not believe in using banks and never wanted the Feds to know how much money he was saving. Furthermore, he did not want the mother of his son Damian to get more than the ten dollars a week he was paying in child support.

Damian was just ten years old, and when I met him for the first time I had just turned seventeen and was in my senior year of high school. The three of us went out to eat at a diner near Jonathan's house, and when Jonathan excused himself to go the bathroom, Damian asked, "How old are you?"

"Seventeen," I said, without fully processing why he would ask such a question.

He nodded his head and continued eating his dinner in silence. It wasn't until a few minutes later that I realized that his mother must have put him up to asking that question. Now that I had spilled the beans, she would know that I was underage. I was embarrassed but did not fully understand why. I told Jonathan what Damian had asked me, and needless to say, he was furious. That was the first and last time I saw Damian up close.

When I asked Jonathan if he had other children, he told me that Damian was his only child, but there was a young man who called him dad because he looked up to him. In fact, they both shared the same first name, but the young man was called JP for short.

"Wow, that is such a coincidence that you and JP are both named Jonathan," I told him. "I guess it was meant to be."

It was a common name, so I thought nothing of it. I saw JP often and, although we were the same age, he had dropped out of high school to pursue a life of a drug dealer. It did not take long for me to figure out that Jonathan was JP's supplier.

I later found out that Jonathan used to be one of the biggest drug dealers in the city. After serving a four-year jail sentence back in the 80s, he went back to hustling on the city buses, doing the shell game and Three Card Monte. However, he was persuaded to get back into the drug game once young JP decided to sell drugs.

Jonathan believed that JP would be better off using his old New York connection and that they both could benefit if he bought pure cocaine by the kilo (one thousand grams), cooked it up, and distributed the crack to JP and his friends. The young men would all give Jonathan a cut off their sales, and every few days or so we would drive to pick up the money and drop off more eight balls of crack. Eight balls were what we called an eighth of an ounce or 3.5 grams of cocaine.

Not only was I hustling with Jonathan on the city buses playing Three Card Monte, but I was also getting paid extra money to go with him to New York to purchase the cocaine. We would drive to the Bronx, take a cab to one of the local Dominican restaurants, and sit down to order some food. A few minutes after placing our order, a stranger would join and chat while they exchanged powder cocaine under the table. The coke would always go into my black messenger bag, and after finishing our food, we would slip away as if we were just having a normal lunch in the city. Each time we made these trips, there was an unspoken rule that hung in the air. If we were to get caught, I would take the charge.

I learned how to cook coke in glass Pyrex cookware and turn it into crack. I also learned how to cut it and weigh out the pieces of crack on a scale, and create eight balls for JP and his crew to sell. I also kept the extra weight at my house along with dismantled guns. All in all, in hindsight, I was just a useful pawn in Jonathan's hustle. Sadly, I somehow believed that living on the edge was a sign of boldness, confidence, and maturity. However, what I was doing with my life at this point was downright dumb.

I was halfway done with my senior year of high school at this point, and I had my entire life ahead of me. In fact, I was signed up with the Army and had completed all the necessary requirements. My recruiter, Sergeant Troy, was confident that I would have a successful career in the military. He had high hopes for me and always encouraged me to stay on target until it was time to leave for boot camp. Sergeant Troy was tall, dark, and handsome. All the girls at my school had a crush on him.

When Sergeant Troy started showing interest in me, I was pleasantly surprised and flattered by his flirtatious ways. One day, he invited me to his house for dinner and a movie and promised to give me a facial and a massage.

"I could see the tension in your body, and I just want to take your mind off things," he said.

I excitedly agreed without any thought as to what Jonathan would do if he found out. I don't remember what I told Jonathan to throw him off my trail, but somehow, I made it to Sergeant Troy's house. As soon as I entered the house, I noticed that he had a massage table. He asked me to lie down, and when I got nice and comfortable, he began massaging my scalp and temples. As he seductively stared into my eyes, I could feel the intensity rising inside me. My breathing got heavy, and all I could think was, "I hope I shaved my legs."

It was about to go down. And then…

Beeeep! Beeeep! Beeeep!

The moment was interrupted because my darn pager was going off! I unclipped the clear pink pager from my belt and glanced at the tiny screen. It only contained three numbers: 111. This was Jonathan's code for emergency or 911. He would always say everyone used 911, so it's hard to tell when there is a real emergency or when someone is just trying to get you to call back right away. Therefore, he created his emergency code. Typical Jonathan — always going against the grain.

I told Sergeant Troy that I had to leave due to an emergency and asked if he could please drop me off at the downtown bus terminal. When we arrived, I hopped out of his car and ran to the nearest pay phone. When I called Jonathan's cell, I was surprised to hear JP's voice instead.

"Dad got bagged by the police!" JP yelled into the phone. "I need you to come down and help me bail him out!"

I just so happened to have saved much of the money I had made working with Jonathan, and I used every penny to get him out of jail that night. Sadly, this would not be the last time I would deplete all of my resources to bail him out.

I met JP and the bail bondsman at the jail, and Jonathan

was released not too long after. He was playing the shell game, and one of the vics called the police and accused Jonathan of robbing them. Lucky for Jonathan, enough eyewitnesses confirmed that the man had not been robbed, but had instead been conned out of his money by playing the game. I was relieved that the situation was not as serious as it could have been.

I had to admit that I had developed serious feelings for Jonathan. However, in hindsight, I don't believe I was in love with him. I had likely confused the excitement and money with being in love with him. I was in love with the idea that I could have whatever I wanted and never worry about where my next dollar was going to come from.

Sex with Jonathan was not even that great. At this point in my life, I still had not experienced an orgasm, so I was only giving him sex because I did not want him to get it elsewhere. Boy, was my logic off. I found out later that not only was he having sex with multiple females, but we were all underage and in high school. In a few months, two of them would be pregnant. I was one of them.

Chapter 10

I'm Pregnant, Again

After having bouts of nausea, vomiting, and craving pickles, I went to a local pharmacy and purchased a pregnancy test. I told my best friend that I thought I was pregnant, but I said it jokingly, hoping that it was not true. I took the test home and beelined to the bathroom. A few minutes later, I was looking at two bold pink lines indicating that I was carrying my third child.

Oh, did I forget to mention that there were two pregnancies and not one that existed before this occurrence? My ex-boyfriend, Juan, and I hooked up again during the early stages of my relationship with Jonathan, and I ended up getting pregnant by Juan for the second time. Now, instead of our mothers forcing us to have an abortion, it was Jonathan.

When I first started dating Jonathan, I felt comfortable telling him that I had a fling with my ex and ended up pregnant. His response was calm but cold.

"Well, let's hurry up and get this baby out of your belly," he said.

I ended up paying for the abortion myself, and this time it was not as evasive as the first experience. I just inserted a few pills inside of me, which induced a miscarriage. It was so easy that it was scary.

Now I was on my third pregnancy, and as scared as I was, I was determined to see this one through. I was so shaken up by the pregnancy test results that I accidentally left it in the bathroom. My mother discovered the test lying on the sink and approached me with it.

"Is this yours?" she asked while holding the test up in the air, as if to say, "exhibit A."

"Yes," I admitted with a look of shame written all over my face. She couldn't force me to have an abortion this time, or so I thought.

She stared at me for a few seconds, shook her head in disgust, and walked away. Well, that went better than I'd imagined. In my mind, I pictured that when she found out she would just start swinging belts, extension cords, purse straps, shoes, pots, pans, and knives. Although my mother was a strict woman, I am sure at this point she figured I was almost done with high school — just a few weeks from graduating — and I would soon be out of the house.

Honestly, after the initial shock, I felt a naive sense of relief. I thought to myself, *I can still go to college in the fall and live on campus.* Luckily, Jonathan had tried to talk me out of going to the military, so I had applied to colleges and even received scholarship awards. I did not regret being pregnant, because in my mind I could never be a statistic if Jonathan would always take care of us. He would make sure that our child would have everything he or she needed, and we would never have to depend on others to help us out.

Soon, I was going to be out of my mother's house, and I could raise my child under my own roof. I had big dreams of living with Jonathan and being a stay-at-home mom, all while completing my college education. The only downside, in my opinion, was that the Army career I had hoped for would never happen. In fact, I still had someone else that I needed to tell — Sergeant Troy.

Sergeant Troy and I never made it to a second date. I am so grateful that things did not go where they could have gone the night of our date. When I would see him at school making his rounds, he would give me a look that said, "You know you owe me, right?" I'm not going to pretend as if I didn't like the teasing and the flirting. But looking back, I have to remind myself that I was still a young girl and he was an adult that should not have been taking advantage of girls my age. However, would he have been a better choice than Jonathan? I'll never know.

All of us teenage girls thought we were mature, and we definitely all thought we could handle adult relationships. However, the truth is this: at that age you just don't know what you don't know. So, because he was still expecting me to leave for boot camp in a couple of weeks, I had to break the news to him that I was not leaving and that I was pregnant.

I had the guidance counselor page Sergeant Troy to the front office. When he arrived, we chose a private room to talk. I am sure he was not ready for what I was about to say.

"So, you wanted to talk? What's up?" Sergeant Troy asked.

"I know it's almost time for me to leave for boot camp," I said. "I appreciate everything that you and the other recruiters have done to get me prepared."

"OK, what are you trying to say?"

"Um… I'm not going to be able to go after all."

"Why?" He sat forward in his seat anxiously looking at me for clarity. He took my hand into his own and stared into my eyes in a way that gave me mixed emotions. Was he a father figure or a lover?

"What happened? Talk to me," he continued.

"I'm pregnant."

Sergeant Troy jumped up out of his seat and paced back and forth, angrily grabbing at his curly hair. He was sexy even when he was angry. I didn't realize just how much my news had affected him until he turned around and faced me. Tears were pouring down his face. I felt like crap.

He sat back down and would not make eye contact with me. He put his head down, and with his face in his hands, he wept like a baby. I didn't know what to say. I hadn't realized that he cared this much. Was it that bad that I was pregnant? I would be in college soon; what was the big deal?

Finally, he looked up at me and said, "How far along are you?"

"I dunno, maybe two months."

"So you're keeping it?"

"I guess."

"Who's the father?"

"He's an older guy. He doesn't go to this school."

"Have you told him?"

"No, I was going to tell him today."

Yup. I had yet to break the big news to Jonathan. My mother knew, which meant it was only a matter of time before everyone in my family knew, and now Sergeant Troy. I needed to tell Jonathan quick, fast, and in a hurry. The truth is, I was sort of scared of what his response would be. It turns out that I had every reason to be concerned.

Later that night, I called Jonathan and told him that I was carrying his baby. I don't know what made me break the news over the phone. His initial response was shocking.

"It ain't mine," he said with an annoying chuckle. "It's probably that half-breed Juan's baby."

"I haven't been with Juan or anyone else," I said. Anger was quickly building up inside of me.

"Well, it ain't mine, so you might as well get rid of it anyway."

With that, he hung up on me.

I called him repeatedly and desperately paged him countless times to no avail. Finally, he called me back the next day. He asked me how I was feeling and if I was hungry and wanted to grab a bite to eat. He sounded genuinely concerned! I wasn't sure what to make of this Dr. Jekyll and Mr. Hyde act, but I agreed to eat with him. We talked it over, and he concluded that he based his initial reaction on fear. He said it caught him off guard and that he was sorry. He made promises always to take care of our child and me, and that we would never have to want for anything.

"I guess things are going to get serious now," he said. "You're stuck with me, Mary Kaye."

"What do you plan on doing with me?" I asked.

"Huh?"

"I said what are you going to do with me? Are you going to keep me?"

In my young mind, I had started to think of myself as a possession to be claimed or tossed aside depending on the mood or intention of the person I was with at the moment. I was placing all control in his hands, and I was not even aware of what I was doing. He never even answered my question. He just looked at me amusingly and pulled me close to him.

As my belly slowly swelled over the summer, I prepared myself physically and mentally to go off to college. We packed everything away and bought some much-needed items for my dorm room. I had everything I could want and need, plus some extra cash from my scholarships. When I moved into my dorm, my family came along to help me get settled in. I met my roommate, Tatiana, for the first time, and we instantly clicked.

When I told her that I was pregnant, she raised her eyebrows in surprise but immediately went back to unpacking her clothes and changed the subject. We talked about everything from Black girl hair problems to our future career goals. She brought the fridge, and I brought the computer. She brought the barrel curling iron, and I brought the flat iron. She brought the television, and I brought the microwave.

After we got everything in its rightful place, we went down to new student orientation. College life was just what I needed. No more hustling, no more cooking coke and selling crack, and my world no longer revolved around Jonathan. Or so I thought.

A few weeks into the college flow, Jonathan inquired about my leftover scholarship money.

"How much they give you?" he asked.

"I have a few thousand left," I said.

"I've been thinking," he said excitedly. "I thought that JP could take that money and flip it. We can get even more coke next time, and I can give you that money right back plus interest."

"Um, I thought I should save it for next semester. You know, just in case."

"You're a brainiac, Mary. You've always been much smarter than your age dictates. I know you realize how much we can make off of this. Plus, you already know I got enough dough to open a bakery, so I got you. What are you worried about, Mary Kaye?"

If I had thought about it, I would have realized that he could have bought his coke with all this "dough" he supposedly had. Yet, here he was asking me if he and JP could borrow it for their next coke run. I agreed to it because, truthfully, we had done this countless times in the past with his money. However, this time I could get a more significant cut. I agreed and gave him two thousand dollars. Unfortunately, before I could see a return on my investment, JP got locked up.

After we bailed JP out, he was forced to lay low until his sentencing. All purchases and sales came to a halt. In fact, it would take almost ten years before I got my money back.

While JP sat on his hands, Jonathan came up with another hustle — rap music. Back in the day, Jonathan was a well-known local rap artist, and an old friend who happened to be a DJ convinced him to get back into the studio. This DJ, who went by the name of BlackStar, also talked him into investing in a local artist named Shadow. Shadow was a ghostwriter for some big names in the industry and wanted to step from behind the scenes and finally release his music. The only problem was that Shadow did not have the finances to invest in studio time.

One evening, I took a break from my studies to go to the studio with Jonathan. When we walked in, I immediately took note of how well-respected he was. Everyone wanted to fill me in on Jonathan's history in the rap game.

"Yo, Jonathan is one of the best cats ever to do it!" said BlackStar. "Have you heard this dude rap?" BlackStar was excited to have someone else witness what he thought was a musical genius. "Def Jam is going to love this new record!" he added.

"Def Jam?" I asked.

Jonathan started smiling from ear to ear. He let out a cool laugh and put his arm around me. "That's what I brought you here to tell you," said Jonathan. "Your man is making moves like shoes, and I refuse to lose."

Apparently, everything he said from now on would rhyme. However, I couldn't help but be anxious about this possible new deal with Def Jam. It had to be huge!

"We had this meeting earlier today with one of the top execs from the record company," said Jonathan. "They want to make a documentary out of my life. They heard that I flow, too, so now they want me to release a couple of tracks and see what kind of buzz I can create."

Jonathan immediately went into attack mode. In fact, he had a role for everyone to play. He hired a couple of young guys to follow him with a camcorder while he hustled in the streets and on the bus. He also went into the studio and quickly recorded a few songs. Soon, we were all busying ourselves stapling posters on every telephone pole we could find in an effort to promote his new single.

The most exciting part for Jonathan was having the boys follow him around with the camera. People everywhere thought he was someone famous, or would just flock to him out of curiosity. His newfound attention also attracted lots of females, but there I was, pregnant and miles away on a college campus far from all the action for the most part.

Chapter 11

Trapped

The next few months were extremely challenging. I was getting physically bigger every week while Jonathan was out there becoming "hood famous." Meanwhile, college life was fun but overwhelming, and it did not take long for me to realize that I would not be able to complete the second semester. My baby was due mid-February, and I planned to go back to school the following fall. When the semester came to a close, I had passed all my classes but was embarrassed to go back to my mother's house.

Jonathan and I decided that it would be best if I moved in with him. However, his apartment was almost an hour from my mother and family. I figured this was only a temporary situation, and while I loved my independence, I secretly hoped that we would eventually move a little closer to my family. After all, Jonathan's apartment contained only one bedroom, and it was just not practical for even a small family.

I moved in with Jonathan during the latter part of December only to have him give me a list of strict rules. The first rule was that I was never to answer his house phone. He set up his house phone in a way so that he could forward all calls to his pager. Furthermore, under no circumstances was I to use the phone or answer it while he was out of the house.

The second rule was that I was never to leave the apartment. He lived in an apartment complex on the fourth floor. If you did not have a key, the exit door would close behind you and lock you out of the building. He further justified not giving me a key by telling me his landlord did not allow tenants to copy keys, and he did not want me going in and out because his landlord might see me and possibly raise his rent.

Rule number three was that I was never to answer the door if anyone knocked, nor was I to reveal that I was inside the apartment.

I complied with all of these rules because I made myself believe that his reasons behind them were valid and sincere. I must admit that it took a lot not to use the house phone because I did not have a cell phone at the time, and it was very boring sitting in the house all day. I felt trapped. I was pregnant and trapped. It had gotten to the point where he would stay out all day and night with the excuse that he was promoting his music and traveling from state to state.

There were some days where he would leave me with very little food in the house. I recall eating plain tuna out of the can with saltine crackers for dinner one night, all because he refused to stock up on food. To get through the day, I would watch one television show after another because it helped the time to go by faster that way. My daily routine went something like this:

7 a.m. – get out of bed and shower
8 a.m. – eat breakfast and watch "Good Morning America"
9 a.m. – watch "Live! With Regis & Kathie Lee"
10 a.m.– watch "Maury"
11 a.m.– watch "The View"
12 p.m. – eat lunch and take a nap
1 p.m.– watch "All My Children"
2 p.m.– watch "One Life to Live"
3 p.m.– take a break
4 p.m.– watch "Maury" (again)
5 p.m.– watch "Ricki Lake"

6 p.m.– watch the local news

7 p.m.– watch "Friends" (two episodes)

8 p.m.– watch the featured sitcom for the evening or a movie

When the evening rolled around, I occupied myself until it was time for dinner and bed. Sometimes Jonathan would be home, and sometimes he would not. When he stayed away for longer periods of time, I would busy myself by looking through his apartment for clues about his real character. I just knew something wasn't right. I was beginning to think that maybe he was not who he said he was.

The first thing I discovered was that his bedroom set contained many hidden compartments. I found everything from extra cash, jewelry, telephone records, pictures of naked girls, letters from his time in prison, etc. I kept looking until I found a few critical things that turned my world upside down.

First, I found a recent photo of him with another female. I could tell it was recent because he was wearing the Tommy Hilfiger shirt and hat set I had bought for him as a Christmas gift only weeks ago! I kept looking. Next, I found one of the videotapes from his recent recordings. I popped in the cassette unsure as to what I would find.

My heart dropped as I watch one of my worst fears unfold on the television screen. Jonathan was with the female from the photo, and she was very pregnant. He kissed her on the cheek and flirtatiously sang to her, telling her that she and their unborn child meant the world to him. She looked to be about seven months pregnant, and it turned out that she was due only a month after me.

Hot tears of anger and heartbreak rolled down my face as I watched my man profess his love for another girl. I furiously started looking through the phone records that I found at the bottom of one of his secret compartments. A few numbers caught my attention, and I realized that the female in the video was likely not the only one he was cheating on me with. However, this was not the worst. Beneath the telephone bills were stacks of child support receipts for three different women. In fact, one of the receipts had JP's name on it!

It was then that I realized Jonathan had lied about JP not being his biological son. Why on earth would someone deny their child like that? Would he do the same thing to me? These questions rushed through my head as I frantically searched through piles of papers. Finally, I came upon an innocent looking doctor's appointment card. However, on the card was Jonathan's name and birth date: 1960.

Wait, he was born in 1960? I couldn't believe my eyes. At that very moment, I realized that Jonathan was not ten years older than me, but twenty-one years older! That explained why he did not want me to know that JP was his son. It would reveal that he was much older than what he had initially let on. Also, the other child support receipt was for a girl named Tracey. I immediately recognized the name because I had met this young lady before.

In fact, Tracey, JP, and I were all only a few months apart in age. When I met Tracey, she was hugging Jonathan around his neck. When I asked him who the female was he was hugged up with, he explained that it was just some girl that had a crush on him. He said she called him "Daddy" as a way of flirting with him. It turns out this was his daughter all along!

It was too much information to handle in just one day. Not only did he have a baby on the way with another female, but he already had three children instead of one. After the two unborn children would arrive into this world, Jonathan would be a father of five. This was not what I signed up for. What was my plan? What could I do at this point?

One of my biggest fears was that Jonathan would refuse to sign our son's birth certificate to hide his true age. Therefore, I made up my mind that I had to tell him that I knew how old he was before having our child. I also wanted him to know that I knew about the other female and his eighteen-year-old son and daughter. First, I had to get out of this prison of an apartment.

The next chance I had I told Jonathan that I wanted to go back to my mom's house. My excuse was that I wanted her to be there when I went into labor. He agreed that this was probably a good move, especially since he was working so hard trying to get a record deal. He claimed Def Jam told him there was a great possibility that he could have his own label, so they suggested that he start working on releasing music independently right away. From there, Jonathan created a record company that he felt would be the beginning of a legit business. With legit money in his pocket, he finally felt comfortable ditching his old GMC Jimmy and purchasing a midnight blue Mercedes.

When he brought me to my mother's house, she finally met the real Jonathan. I don't think she ever realized that this was not the same guy she met what seemed like ages ago, because by this time I had completed my first semester of college and I was almost nine months pregnant. When she met him, she knew he was older, and when she asked me his age, I was too embarrassed to tell her. I gave her the same answer that I once thought to be the truth.

"He's only twenty-eight," I lied.

"Twenty-eight?!" she exclaimed. "How in the world you end up with a twenty-eight-year-old man, and you JUST turned eighteen?"

"Mommy, I didn't know how old he was at first. He treats me good; and he has a lot of money."

I wanted to confess everything to her and cry in her lap. I wanted to tell her how I was scared of having his baby, and how he had two children who were also eighteen, in addition to his young son Damian who was now eleven years old. I also wanted to confess that I had found out that there was another baby on the way. Finally, I tried to tell her that Jonathan was not twenty-eight and that he was really thirty-nine-years-old! However, I was too ashamed to say anything. I suffered in silence. I felt like my life should have been just beginning, but instead, it seemed to be crashing all around me.

Chapter 12

Struggling to Be Happy

My mother and oldest sister planned a baby shower for me that turned out to be the most fun I had experienced in a very long time. I remember that day like it was yesterday. Sitting in that chair with my belly out to my knees, and wearing my Central Connecticut State University hoodie to hold on to my last bit of college life experience.

The baby shower was a major blessing. I received everything I needed and then some. It should have been a sign to me that Jonathan was not my source of support. Unfortunately, my pride would not let me admit to everyone that I was wrong about him. I desperately wanted this relationship to work, and I wanted to be the one to reap the benefits of being his lady. What if he got signed to Def Jam? What if his career took off? What if I am walking away from a gold mine? Apparently, fortune and fame carried so much weight in my mind that I was willing to sacrifice my happiness for it. The truth is, I was miserable.

However, I still had to confront Jonathan about his age. I was still afraid that he would not sign the birth certificate to avoid revealing his exact age. Finally, during his visit to see me after a long day of hustling, I broke the news. "A few weeks ago I saw something at the house," I said nervously while looking down at my bed.

The comforter had a blue and white flower pattern on it that matched the curtains my mother had made for my bedroom. I started picking at one of the pieces of loose threads as I said, "It had your birthdate on it."

I looked up at his face to see his reaction. Poker face.

"And?" he said.

"And it said you were born in 1960," I said. "I thought you were twenty-eight."

"Aww, Bootie," he said, calling me by my childhood nickname. "You knew all this time and didn't say anything? Wow, you are too smart for your own good."

He pinched my cheek, chuckled, and kissed my forehead. "I can't believe you knew all this time, and you still want to be with me. That's why I love you."

He went into this long speech, half talking and half rapping his way back into my heart. He went on and on about how he was afraid that if I knew, I would change my mind about him, and how he wanted to spend the rest of his life with me.

"See, I'm not like these young cats that's out here just trying to get what's in between your legs," he said. "I'm trying to get what's in between your ears. If I grab hold of your heart and your mind, all the rest of that stuff is going to fall right behind."

If I weren't so hurt and depressed, I probably would have found his speech comical.

"You got the brain of a forty-year-old lady," he continued. "That's why you were able to bag me so quick. I always knew there was something special about you, Mary Kaye."

After he finished praising my forty-year-old brain, and ability to bag the "flyest OG" in Connecticut, I realized this was the perfect opportunity to confront him about the other pregnant female.

"There is something else I wanted to ask you," I said. "Are you cheating on me?"

Stupid question. I had weeks to prepare for this moment, and I opened the conversation like this?

"Huh? What makes you ask that?"

"Because I know you have someone else pregnant. Are y'all together or something?"

He looked away and shook his head "no."

"Nah, she's just somebody I had working with me for a minute while you were in school," he explained. "That bitch knew what she was doing 'cause I told her you was pregnant."

He claimed that the girl didn't tell him she was having a baby until she was almost six months into the pregnancy. He implied that he would have made her get an abortion and that somehow, she seduced *him* into having sex with her.

"When is she due?" I asked.

"Around the second week of March, I think."

"What's her name?"

"Treneice. Why? She don't mean nothing," he said. "She's gonna have that baby, and then I am going to make sure we get a paternity test."

"One more thing," I said. I was nowhere near done with him, but I was already mentally and physically exhausted. "I know JP and Tracey are your kids."

His mouth dropped open, and he let out a loud laugh. He had this laugh that would start out as an actual laugh but then taper off into a snicker. I hated it.

"You were holding all of this in? Yo, you ain't even shed not one tear this whole time," he said, looking at me in amazement.

He had no clue that I had been crying myself to sleep almost every night. By this time, I think my body had released every bit of liquid emotion it could muster.

"I didn't want you to know because I didn't think you could handle it," he said. "Honestly, I've always questioned if

Tracey was mine, but I promised to take care of her, so I did."

"Do you still wonder if you're the father of the baby I am carrying?"

"I would never do that, Bootie."

Too late, since he already denied our child when I first told him I was pregnant. I suppose that slipped his mind.

Our son was due to be born on February 18, 2000. However, I went into labor the day after Valentine's Day, and after twenty-one hours of labor, I gave birth to a beautiful eight pounds seven ounce baby boy. Jonathan insisted that we name our son after him, and I happily agreed to it, because it was a sign that Jonathan would never deny our son again. He signed the birth certificate, of course, and there it was in black and white: Father: Jonathan _________, thirty-nine years old.

When it was time for the hospital to release me, Jonathan was there. However, I went back to my mother's house so that she could help me during Jonathan Jr.'s infant stages. I fell in love with my baby. I would lie in bed at night and just stare into his big, round eyes. I thought my life was over, but my Junior gave me an indescribable feeling of hope and newfound joy.

One night when he was around three months old, I looked at him, and he smiled at me. I responded by smiling back and making a noise, which he repeated. We went back and forth doing that until he would burst out laughing. Eventually, he fell asleep. This became our bedtime ritual every night. We kept at this until one day he got very sick. Junior had developed a fever that just wouldn't go away.

I took him to the doctor and they gave him a prescription, but the medicine didn't work. Within a few days, his eyes became bloodshot red, and he developed a rash on his arms and torso. I called Jonathan and told him we needed to take Junior back to the doctor. He said he was in the middle of something important. When I lashed out at him about his son being more important than whatever he was doing, he cussed me out and hung up the phone. With tears in my eyes, I called for a cab and took my son to the emergency room.

They ended up admitting Junior, and after running multiple tests, the doctor finally came up with a diagnosis: Kawasaki Disease. I had never heard of such a thing. I called my mother and told her what the doctors said, and she immediately left work early and rushed to the hospital. Jonathan still hadn't shown up. My mother started praying over Junior, and when she finished, she reassured me that he was going to be all right. She made some phone calls and discovered that a friend of the family had a child diagnosed with the same disease. It had affected the baby's heart in such a way that heart surgery was needed. We prayed that our circumstances would be different.

Thankfully, the doctors reported that Junior's heart was not affected, but as a precaution, they prescribed him Bayer Aspirin and iron medicine. Unfortunately, the fever was still quite high, and they could not figure out how to get it to go down. The doctors decided to transfer him to a nearby hospital that was better equipped to handle situations like this. After two days in the new hospital, the fever subsided, and he was allowed to go home.

I was so grateful that my son was OK. The doctors said that Junior's recovery was a miracle. He would not have to remain on Bayer Aspirin for the rest of his life, like some children with the same disease. He would only need to take half an aspirin for a few weeks. Also, his heart was still unaffected by the disease. However, I was disappointed at how Jonathan handled our son's medical scare. I recommitted myself to making the most of every opportunity instead of waiting for Jonathan to create a life for us, so I re-enrolled in college.

I went to the local community college and took on just two classes so that I could also work an overnight shift as a pharmacy technician at a local Walgreens. Jonathan took note that I was becoming more and more independent, so he did everything he could to discourage me from working. My mother did not have a car at the time, and he refused to bring me to work at night. I was so determined that I found a cab driver that would give me a special weekly rate for pick-ups and drop-offs to and from my job.

When my son needed to go to the doctor, I would use the same cab driver or take the city bus. Now and then, while taking the bus, I would see Jonathan at the bus terminal still hustling and promoting his music. He would pause and gush over his son and tell everyone how he was a father and every dime he made was going to his seed.

"I'm a stack maniac, an OG brainiac, and I ain't holding nothing back!" he would rap while trying to urge people to bet their hard-earned money.

I must admit, the crowd loved his anecdotes and impromptu rhymes. I would be lying if I said I didn't find it oddly charming as well. I got caught up in the paper chase and ended up with a baby by this charismatic hustler. Behind the scenes, I was struggling to be happy. I was working hard to save my own money and get an education. All the while, most of my money was going toward helping my mother around the house and paying for transportation to and from work and school. Because I enrolled in college part time, I did not qualify for financial aid, so I was also paying for college. It gave me some sense of peace though.

It was better than depending on a man to take care of me; that was for sure. In fact, I finished that semester on the Dean's List, and I was proud of myself. Things were going well on my job, and I soon got used to working all night and stealing sleep throughout the day while my son napped. When Christmas rolled around, I was still at my mom's house, and she didn't seem to mind. She had four bedrooms and always seemed to have a house full of people. On Christmas day, Jonathan stopped by and, after spending some time playing with our son, he called my mom into the living room.

He pulled out a small red box, opened it up, and revealed a solitary diamond ring. "Mommy, I want to spend the rest of my life with this woman," he said. Then he turned to me and kneeled down at my feet.

"I've had so many women it could break a calculator, but it's seriously time for me to settle down and I want to make you the happiest woman on this planet. No more games."

He slipped the ring onto my finger and asked, "Will you marry me?"

I hugged him so tight you would have thought I was clinging to him for my very life! He had truly caught me off guard, and I wanted nothing more than to prove everyone wrong. I still don't know if love was a major part of the equation. The thought of being married to the father of my child was something that I had wanted for some time now. I refused to be a statistic. There were too many young black mothers, but not enough black wives. Now, when I pushed my son's stroller through the mall, I could do it with pride because of the ring that now rested on my left hand.

That evening my mother painted my fingernails bright red, because I couldn't go to work that night showing off my ring without my nails done. My co-workers gushed over my little quarter karat diamond ring. I knew it was small, but I loved it. I knew with all the money he had that he would eventually get me something bigger and better. It was a start.

Chapter 13

A Welcomed Distraction

Following our engagement, Jonathan talked more about our future together, but, interestingly, he showed up less and less. I was still at my mother's house and too busy working and taking care of our son to care about what he was doing. Plus, I was still enrolled in college taking just one class for the spring semester. I had even started dressing more stylishly thanks to Alexa, a close friend of mine. She kept reminding me that I needed to get rid of the navy blue, brown, and black clothes in my closet, and brighten up my wardrobe.

"You have this huge closet, with six items in it," Alexa observed. "Why?"

"I dunno," I said. "I wear my black or blue pants to work, and my white shirts go with both. The blue jacket goes with everything, and I love my brown sweater."

"Oh no, we need to go shopping ASAP. I'm not about to have you out here looking a hot mess this summer."

Alexa and I went to a local department store, and I picked out a red belt and red sandals to start. I figured the bold color could brighten up items I already owned.

"OK, now you got potential," she said, "but you still need to get rid of those glasses. Your glasses are saying 'Anne Klein' but your outfit is saying 'Forever 21.' You need to get you some contact lenses or something!"

I took heed to every word of fashion advice Alexa could muster. Soon, I invested in some contact lenses and chucked the glasses. A wide variety of department stores started selling their inventory online, so I took full advantage and shopped for some designer items. When Alexa came by to pick me up one day, I had on a pair of chunky sandals, a knee-length asymmetrical jean skirt, a Dolce & Gabbana tank top, and Chanel shades. Alexa beamed like a proud mama.

As the temperature started rising into the high nineties, we made it a weekend ritual to ride through the local park in her Jeep. The big thing to do that summer was to ride through the park at about five miles an hour until you saw someone worth stopping for. Guys beeped their car horns at us and told us how cute we were. Friends would call out to Alexa to pull over, and our haters would roll their eyes and pretend not to see us.

One thing I liked about this routine was that it was breaking me out of my comfort zone. I needed to know that there were other possibilities for happiness in life. I needed to know that the world did not revolve around Jonathan. I knew he was out there cheating, but I turned a blind eye and found a release in my friendship with Alexa. She could see that Jonathan was controlling me, and she urged me to speak up for myself. However, I just couldn't bring myself to do it.

No matter how much she tried to boost my self-esteem, I still felt like damaged goods. I felt used up and felt as if a teenager with a baby boy was not desirable to the men we came in contact with.

However, Alexa reminded me that she had a son around the same age as mine, and that didn't stop her from enjoying life. We both had our pre-baby bodies back, and although we were not into the club scene, we just enjoyed passing the time by looking cute in her Jeep.

I took one class that summer to make up for the one I did not take in the spring. I still did not have my driver's license, but Jonathan began renting cars to take on the road to preserve the life of his new Mercedes. Now and then he would let me use one of the cars to get back and forth to work. It was a small consolation for the constant heartache he was putting me through.

By this time, he had gotten another teenager named Tynika pregnant, and she gave birth to her child that year. I was devastated that he would do this yet again. I hacked into his voicemail account and heard messages from multiple females, and I could tell just by listening to them that he was having sex with all of them. I turned my attention away from Jonathan and started only viewing him as a means to obtain transportation and good weed.

Finally, I felt like I was living. I thought this must be the life of an independent woman, although I was still living at home with my mother. I kept my job as a pharmacy technician until later that fall. The weather started to break, and I had found a job working as a data entry clerk for a large insurance company. The transition seemed like a no-brainer because I went from making ten dollars an hour to twelve dollars an hour.

However, there were a few complications that came with the new job. Tyrone, an old friend from high school, started working there during the same time. He was a hypersexual porn addict that knew how to make me laugh. In fact, he had me laughing all the way to the bedroom, and before I knew it, my mind was far from Jonathan.

Tyrone was a welcome distraction. However, he was a destructive distraction that proved to be the last thing I needed at the time. He was young and exciting, but he still lived at home with his mom and had an off-again/on-again jealous baby mother.

"Yo, Kaye! What we gettin' into tonight?" Tyrone would frequently ask. "We gon' smoke out or what?"

We spent many days and nights smoking that good weed Jonathan kept supplying. He had no clue as to what I was doing with the weed, and I did my best to keep it that way. I started selling some of the weed to my co-workers, and even the vending machine guy that would visit the office once a week.

"What you got this week, Kaye? Hydro? Purple Haze?" Tyrone asked, referring to the different types of potent weed at my disposal.

We routinely booked hotel rooms on the weekend just to have a place to smoke weed and hang out. As a precaution, we would wet a few towels and roll them up at the base of the door to prevent the smell of weed smoke from escaping the room. One day after smoking a few blunts, I looked up at the smoke detector in the hotel room and came to a startling realization.

"We are trying to keep the smoke in the room, but won't the smoke make the smoke detector and the sprinklers go off?" I asked in a panicked voice.

I stood up and pointed to the white circle on the ceiling above the bed. Tyrone looked at me, looked at the blunt in his hand, and took a long drag before blowing long billows of smoke through his wide nostrils.

"Nah, Kaye. If that were gonna happen, it would have happened already," he chuckled.

"But… what if it's a silent alarm?"

I stood on the bed and started furiously fanning the smoke detector. After a few minutes, Tyrone passed me the blunt, and while standing a few inches beneath it, I blew a puff of smoke right at the thing! It suddenly occurred to me how ridiculous the whole thing was, and we burst out laughing.

I laughed until my sides began to hurt and tears were streaming down my face. Tyrone laughed at my silliness, and as I fell back onto the pillow gasping for breath from my bouts of uncontrollable laughter, he tugged at my legs and pulled me to the edge of the bed.

"I'm mad horny, Kaye. I'm ready to bang out."

He always demanded sex from me as if I were obligated to give it to him. He always treated me like my entire worth would rise and fall on how good I was at pleasing him sexually. To be honest, I willingly allowed him to treat me like this. I received a strange sense of satisfaction out of letting him think he was in control when truthfully, I had all the power in the relationship. Looking back on the situation, I was giving my body and my mind away at a very cheap cost.

I convinced myself that I chose to be this man's sex toy and that I got just as much out of the deal as he did. My foolish goal was to make Tyrone feel like a king, all while making myself feel like a cheap whore. I thought I was having fun. I thought I was escaping what felt like a slow death with Jonathan. The reality was that I had exchanged one prison cell for another.

One day, Tyrone and I were involved in an accident while driving to work in his mother's car. Another vehicle struck the side of the car while he was attempting to change lanes. The responding police officer determined that Tyrone was at fault. This worried him because the car was new (just a few months old) and he had already ruined his car privileges with his mom.

Beginning the next pay period, Tyrone's checks went straight to his mom to pay off the car insurance deductible. His dilemma began an ongoing process of Tyrone borrowing money from me for train fare, breakfast, lunch, blunts, and whatever else he needed while we were together.

"Yo, I promise I got you, Kaye," he continually reminded me.

"How long before the deductible is paid off?" I asked.

"A few more weeks, and then I'm straight."

I waited patiently, and after a few weeks he came up with another excuse. "Baby mom is asking me to pay the daycare center so she can work. She wants to save her money to get her car out of the shop."

A few more weeks went by.

"Mom is asking me to help pay rent, or she gonna make me move out. I'm not trying to go live at my baby mom's right now."

After a few months of IOU's, Tyrone owed me well over twelve hundred dollars. It was nearing Christmas season, and I had my own obligations to take care of. My money was going fast trying to help Tyrone during his "hardships," and I needed to figure out a way to get some extra money.

A few people on my job knew I was a booster, so I began taking orders for Christmas gifts. There was a local store that had everything anyone could want so they would make a list, and I would bring back the items in exchange for cash. Things were going so well that I convinced Tyrone that we should quit our jobs.

I was tired of working just to give him a third of my paycheck anyway. One day I convinced him to just walk out together without saying anything. I knew that our co-workers thought I was following his lead instead of the other way around, but I didn't care. I was making more money boosting than sitting at a desk for forty hours a week anyway.

While shoplifting, I would even steal things for Tyrone and his daughter. He wore the latest clothes and Timberland boots because of my boosting capabilities. Somewhere along the way, he started getting cocky.

"Yo, Kaye. Come pick me up," he said. He was calling from somewhere on the west side of town and needed a ride back home.

When I arrived at the address, I honked the horn a few times with no response. I got out of the car and rang the doorbell. After a few minutes, Tyrone opened the door and invited me inside. I could tell he was high because his face looked puffy and his eyes were bloodshot red. He had a goofy look on his face.

"You got smoked out without me, huh?" I asked.

"Come upstairs. My boy got some more if you want some."

Just as he promised, his friend had more weed, so I stayed for a few minutes to smoke with them. I ended up staying longer than expected because I wanted to come down off the high a little before getting behind the wheel to take Tyrone home. Tyrone's friend, Rico, offered me a drink. I turned down the offer because I didn't want to stay much longer.

Rico looked at Tyrone and said, "Is this you?"

He was asking him if we were a couple.

"Nah man, we just cool. She cool peoples."

Rico looked at me and said, "You mad pretty. What you doing hanging with this dude?"

"Thank you," I said. "Like Ty said, that's my boy."

"What are you? Are you mixed or something?"

I rolled my eyes and laughed at his question; without responding, I told Tyrone that we had to go. Although Tyrone and I weren't in an exclusive relationship, by this time he had confessed his love for me. It caught me off guard to hear him openly downplay what I thought we had.

"Wait up. Just stay a few minutes," Rico said.

By this time, Rico was approaching me. He was giving me a look that told me he didn't want me to leave because he wanted more than just my company. I glanced at Tyrone, and to my surprise, he did not seem to care about what was taking place. In fact, he seemed amused by his friend's behavior. Before I realized what was happening, Tyrone and Rico exchanged a look that should have revealed that they were up to no good. When I stood up to head for the door, Tyrone grabbed me from behind in a bear hug and carried me into his friend's bedroom. At first, I thought he was joking around, and while I was kicking and screaming for him to stop, I was also laughing it all off.

I laughed until Tyrone dropped backward onto Rico's bed with me on top of him. Rico had followed us into the room and was suddenly in front of me. He grabbed my legs and tried to gain control of me. Suddenly, I realized how vulnerable I was with Tyrone holding my arms down, and Rico gripping my legs near my knees. Fear crept into my throat. I screamed, but somehow nothing came out.

Chapter 14

Violated

Rico quickly unbuttoned my jeans and aggressively pulled them down in spite of my violent kicks. My movements were now restricted, with my pants around my knees. Before I knew it, Rico had lifted my legs and quickly thrust himself inside me. He kept thrusting in and out despite my now audible screams while Tyrone held me down from behind. At one point, Tyrone attempted to penetrate me anally while Rico was inside me, but my struggling prevented him from succeeding. As a result, I experienced excruciating pain that I can never fully describe.

Tyrone and Rico had violated and humiliated me in a way that I had never experienced. I had been raped a few times before, but this was different. I thought I could trust them. There I was, being raped right in front of someone I loved while he got some sick sense of pleasure from it all.

At some point, Rico's hands went to my mouth to stifle my screams. My teeth ripped into the inside of my mouth. I could taste blood and weed. My legs began to shake as they were pressed against Rico's chest and positioned almost directly in front of my face.

Finally, Rico climaxed inside me, pulled himself out, pulled up his pants, and rushed downstairs and out of the house, leaving Tyrone and me in the bedroom. Before I could even say anything, Tyrone let me go and jumped to his feet. I slumped to the floor on my hands and knees.

"Yo, that was crazy! Kaye, you are sexy as hell," Tyrone exclaimed. "I've never done anything like that in my life!"

I was appalled that he not only saw nothing wrong with what just took place, but that he thought that I consented to it as well. How could he not see that this was wrong? Sadly, I was too embarrassed about the entire incident to say anything about it. I was worried that I would look stupid for allowing myself to get raped.

Tyrone seemed to be overly excited about what they had just done and kept praising me for being cool with it. I couldn't believe what I was hearing. Eventually, to make myself feel better, I convinced myself that I wanted it. I was still a teenager but had so many sexual partners that it didn't matter that there was one more guy to add to the list, right?

Rico was just one more guy, one more fling, and that would be it. However, my tears told me different. My emotions told me different. My ripped-open vagina, sore from being dry through the entire ordeal, definitely told me different.

I drove Tyrone home in silence. He got out of the car and looked back at me with a silly smirk on his face. I pulled off without saying a word. On the way home, my mind kept replaying the event over and over until I convinced myself that I would never tell anyone what had happened. I feared that Rico would tell everyone anyway, and I would be labeled as a ho. Here I was trying to get revenge on Jonathan and ended up getting raped. I thought my power would come from owning the situation, and getting what I wanted out of it.

Sometime after, I called Tyrone and told him that I wanted to have a threesome with him and Rico. However, this time I wanted to be in control. We booked a hotel room, got drunk, and smoked all of my weed. Not surprisingly, the threesome was not all that enjoyable. I couldn't bring myself to be turned on by these two overly arrogant jackasses, but I put on a good show just to save face. I didn't want to admit that Tyrone was a worthless piece of crap and that I had just willingly given up what was previously taken from me. I wanted to believe that I was sexually liberated, and old enough to sleep with whomever I wanted. If this is what sexual freedom felt like, I didn't want it.

Shortly after this incident, I ended my relationship with Tyrone. It was much easier than I thought it would be. One day, he called my mom's house to vent about his baby mother. She threatened to leave him for good, and his response to her was, "I got bitches sucking the cum out of my dick like a straw and will fuck whoever I want them to fuck, and you think I need you?"

I knew he was talking about me, and it felt like a slap in the face. At that moment, I realized what I was to him. I realized that no matter how much I pretended to be in control, Tyrone's perception was that he had me at his disposal. It wasn't fun anymore. I was done.

"You think you got me like that, huh?" I asked.

"Yup. If I tell you to come over and get me right now, you would."

"Actually, I wouldn't." I couldn't believe these words were coming out of my mouth.

"Yes, you would Kaye. Stop playing."

Silence.

"Come get me," he demanded. "I wanna bang out."

And with that last comment, I hung up the phone. It was the first time I felt true power. I did not always have to be the one to give in. I could say no, and it felt amazing. I could take control of my feelings and desires, and do what Mary wanted to do. At that moment, I wanted nothing else to do with Tyrone.

With this newfound sense of confidence, I felt I could now handle Jonathan. I could stand up to him and deal with him as the father of my child and nothing more. But somewhere deep down I wanted to be with the father of my child, to marry him, and to prove all the girls wrong that thought they could have him by having his baby.

The relationship I had with Jonathan was definitely on the rocks, but I thought I could at least start to ease back into a sense of normalcy with him. I started hustling with him again to gain some extra money because I had to put my boosting on hold after a near run-in with the law. One of the easiest things to do at that point was to hold Jonathan's drugs and guns again. He was supposed to pay me one hundred dollars a week to hide the guns and to weigh and bag eight balls of crack cocaine. However, he would always promise to pay me the next week, and the next, and so on.

I took his word for it because I knew he had the money at his disposal. However, I kept reminding myself that he still owed me thousands of dollars from borrowing my scholarship money. I was such a sucker. I was still living at home with my mother at the time, and I knew I was taking a risk because it was rare that anything got past this woman. One day, my worst fear came true. While cleaning and changing the furniture around in my bedroom, she found the drugs and the dismantled guns.

"What in the world are you thinking?" she yelled. "What's wrong with you? Don't you know one of these kids could have found these drugs and thought it was candy?" She held the tiny pieces of crack in her hand as evidence.

I remained silent. At that point, she would have used anything that I said or did against me. My mother was no joke. I was almost twenty years old at the time, but I knew she could smack the mess out of me at any given moment if I said the wrong thing. She stood there waiting for me to answer. When she saw that I had nothing to say, she shook her head and took the contraband into her room. She fussed all the way there.

"I know it ain't nobody's mess but Jonathan's," she said. "Wait until I see him. Got this junk in my house. What if the cops decided to follow him around and end up raiding my house? You could mess around and make me lose my Section 8! Matter of fact, get out! I don't care where you go, get out! And this mess here," she said holding up a bag of crack. "I'm flushing this down the toilet, too!"

As strict as my mother was, I never expected this. I never thought she would put me out of her house. The only place I could go was back to Jonathan, but I did not want to do that. I wasn't ready to deal with the cheating, the lying, and the two newborn babies that he just had. He made me a public joke, and I just didn't love him anymore. I'm not sure if I ever did.

My mother was serious. She wanted me out. She watched me pack up my belongings along with my son's clothes, diapers, and supplies into my blue 1990 Dodge Shadow and drive off. I had nowhere to go. I called two of my aunts, but those prospects dried up quickly. Neither one of them had any space for my son and me. I wasn't too worried though. Although I didn't want to, I would call Jonathan and just move back in with him.

I had a few dollars in my pocket and some weed. I sold the weed to someone from my old job and was able to get something to eat for the night. Sadly, all I could think about was whether or not Jonathan would be angry with me for having his drugs thrown away. Sure enough, that was his main concern when I called him from a pay phone.

"She flushed my stuff down to the toilet?!" he screamed into the phone.

"I didn't think she would find it. I had it in a good spot!"

"Yeah, but that's mad money I just lost. You do realize I'm not going to pay you that money I owe you, right?"

I was too embarrassed to tell him that my mom had kicked me out. I didn't want him to know that I had nowhere else to go.

He continued. "And another thing. Don't think I don't know about you and that dude Tyron or Tyrone or whatever the hell his name is."

I felt like someone had slapped me across my face. I was tempted to hang up the phone and end this nightmare, but I just stood there holding the phone to my ear. Finally, I said, "What are you talking about? That's my friend from high school."

"You think I'm stupid, Mary Kaye? You had this nigga in my car, smoking my weed; and the sad part is that this nigga played you. Oh, you didn't think I knew?"

I tried to explain to him that I was upset about him having two babies with two different females behind my back. I was tired of how he treated me, how he would cuss me out at the drop of a hat, and how he made me feel like a child.

"OK, we already been down this road before though," he said. "Tell me why this dude was just downtown at the bus terminal bragging about how you let him and his friend run a train on you."

It felt like a ton of bricks just landed on my chest. "What?" I asked weakly. It was all I could muster out.

"See? You didn't even know? That's what you get. Trying to get back at me and you played yourself."

He started laughing at me. I hated his laugh.

I burst into tears, crying out because I knew he was right. I let the phone drop and buried my face in my hands. Why was this happening to me? When I picked up the phone again, I thought my obvious brokenness must have worn him down because he had stopped laughing. However, when he spoke again, his voice was filled with hatred.

"As much I had feelings for you and trusted you, these other females would have never played themselves as you did," he said. "I could call any one of them up right now and tell them to walk down Whalley Avenue butt naked, and they'll do it."

I put another quarter in the pay phone to keep the call going. The tears just wouldn't stop flowing. I was gasping for breath, all the while urging myself to tell him what really happened. I wanted to tell him I had been raped, but something in me was afraid that he would think I was lying. I didn't know what to do. I couldn't think; I couldn't talk. I didn't even realize that Jonathan was still cussing me out on the other end.

"You stupid bitch! I should have never trusted you in the first place." Click.

I had to get back to my son who was waiting only a few feet away in the car. It was cold outside, and I didn't realize how bad I was shivering. I made my way back into the driver's seat and fell apart. It felt like the sky was caving in. I couldn't believe this was happening to me. My mother had kicked me out, and now Jonathan didn't want anything to do with me.

Chapter 15

Homeless

I used the last of my money to get a hotel room. I negotiated a forty-five-dollar rate at this sleazy motel, but at least I had my own pillows and comforter for my son and me to sleep on. The next day, reality set in. What was I going to do? I called my mom and asked her if I could come back home. She hung up on me before I could even finish my first sentence.

I had to check out or pay for an additional night, and since I had no more money, I had no choice but to leave. I contacted the local shelters, but every place I called was filled. I felt defeated. This was a low place that I never thought I would have to see. However, here I was. Desperate.

Everything I owned was in my trunk and back seat of my car, with a sheet covering it. I would have slept in the car, but it was wintertime and spring was nowhere in sight. Thankfully, I had WIC, which was a program that was an acronym for "Women, Infants, and Children." They provided vouchers for healthy foods and baby formula. WIC at least allowed me to get cereal, milk, cheese, peanut butter, and other foods. However, things went from bad to worse when the heat stopped working in my car.

Looking back, I probably just needed coolant, but I had no clue as to why cold air was blowing through the vents. I stopped at a local mechanic that I had known since high school. He had fixed my brakes in the past and seemed to be an honest guy. When I pulled up at his shop, he took one glance at my belongings piled in the back seat and asked what was going on with me. I explained the story in half-truths, and let him know that I was in a very tight situation.

"Honestly, I'm trying to get a hotel room, but I don't have any money," I confessed.

"I tell you what. Let me take care of the hotel room for you and your son tonight," the mechanic said. "I can't have y'all out here in the cold in the middle of the night. Let me get this heat working in your car, and then I'll follow you and get you situated. We can work something out later."

Wow, what a blessing! He was right; it was far too cold for my son and me to be stranded somewhere without a place to stay. I was so grateful when we pulled up at the hotel; I felt like I had a guardian angel. I followed him to the front desk where he paid for the room with his credit card. To my surprise, he paid for a week's stay, which was much more than I expected.

He walked us to the room and made sure that we settled in. I thanked him for his kindness, spread out my blanket, and settled my now fast asleep son on the bed. When I turned around to walk him to the door, I noticed that not only was his coat off and thrown over one of the chairs, but he had also lit up a cigarette as well.

"Oh, I thought you were about to leave," I said.

"Well, I was thinking that since your son is sleeping, we might be able to work out that arrangement."

I played dumb. "Oh, I'm going to try to get some money from my son's father tomorrow, so I can start paying you back."

"No need to worry about that. I don't need any money," he said. "Come over here for a second. I want to get a good look at you."

I walked over to him. My body was shaking. I hated that I was always so nervous. As scared as I was, I hoped he wouldn't notice. I also hoped he would just leave. Besides, I was on my period, so I knew I could at least get through most of this week without having sex with this man.

He took my hand and started massaging the back of it with his thumb. "You've really grown into a beautiful young lady, you know that?" he said in a frighteningly soft, soothing voice.

He stood up and tilted his head toward the bathroom, silently asking me to go in there with him.

"I'm on my period. I can't."

"Do you have on a pad or a tampon?"

"A tampon," I said, puzzled by his question.

"Take it out for me."

He raised his eyebrows knowingly, as if challenging me to admit that I didn't know what was going to happen the moment they swiped his credit card at the front desk.

"Come on," he said, motioning toward the bathroom. "We're wasting time."

He chuckled. I felt sick to my stomach.

"I can pay you," I pleaded. I tried to pull my hand away, but he held on tighter and pulled me closer to him.

"I told you I don't want your money." He stopped smiling, stared me in the eye, and his voice became serious. "Hurry up, before you wake up your son."

I looked back at my son, sleeping on the bed. He was the most beautiful child I had ever seen. I did not know how I was going to get out of this mess I was in. I feared that if I didn't go into the bathroom, he would rape me with my son right there on the bed. What if he woke up?

I reluctantly walked into the bathroom. I felt uneasy about leaving my son in the room with this man, so I left the door open as I quickly pulled off my clothes. Might as well hurry up and get this over with, I thought. I carefully removed my tampon and waited.

When he came into the bathroom, he already had his pants off and was fully erect. He was only wearing his red lumberjack shirt and socks. I thanked God under my breath that he was wearing a condom. I stood against the sink as a trickle of blood streamed down my leg.

He seemed unfazed by this, because he grabbed a few towels and placed them on the floor. Before I could protest, he turned my body around and pushed me to the floor by pressing his hand on my shoulders and back. I started to cry. Part of me wanted to own the situation and pretend I wanted it. "Just enjoy it, Mary," I thought. "It'll be over before you know it."

Because of the blood, he was able to slide right in. I had never had sex with my period before, so I was surprised that there wasn't a bigger mess at first. However, as he got more excited, he became more aggressive. Before I knew it, blood was everywhere. He grabbed at everything on my body that he could possibly grab. He even squeezed at the sides of my face and pressed my cheeks together so hard that I could barely see. He pulled me by my hair, turned me around, and slammed the back of my head against the floor.

I felt like I was going to pass out. He squeezed the sides of my face again, this time forcing my mouth open. Just when I felt like my teeth were going to break under the pressure, he hogged spit directly into my mouth. Finally, he let go. But he wasn't done yet. Up to this point, I thought I had experienced fear, but this was another level of fear. All I could think about was my son. I stifled every cry that crept into my throat out of fear that I would wake him up. The only sound you could hear was the hum of the bathroom vent and his demonic sounding grunts and groans.

When it was all over, there was blood on the wall, on the floor, and all over my lower body. Still breathing heavily, he washed himself off and got dressed. He lit another cigarette, and after taking a drag, he pointed it at me.

"I'll be back to see you tomorrow," he said, "but I'm taking your car so that I can check it out and make sure everything is running right, sweetie."

Sweetie? I felt like a cheap whore. Why did it seem like guys got so much pleasure out of humiliating me? Why did it seem like every guy I have been with since my first boyfriend only wanted sex if they took it through manipulation and control? I soaked my pillow with tears that night. I wondered what in the world I would do. When I woke up the next day, I realized I had no car, no means of transportation to get far away from there. I just watched television all day long to keep my mind off what was bound to take place that night. I knew he was coming back, and I felt helpless at the very thought.

Like clockwork, he returned every night at seven o'clock. By the time the week was over, my body felt like I had been in a car wreck. However, I felt emotionally numb. My movements had become almost robotic. I was getting through each day telling myself that when he finally gave me my car back, I would pack up, leave, and never look back.

Chapter 16

Some Things Never Change

I called Jonathan the moment I got my car keys back from the mechanic. Jonathan seemed like a savior compared to being raped every night. I told him I was sorry, and that if he would please just let me make it up to him, I promised that he could trust me.

He asked me to meet him at the bus terminal to get some gas money. He gave me the keys to his apartment and told me to wait for him until he got home. When he got home that night, Jonathan wrapped his arms around my shoulders and pulled me close to him. He lifted up my chin with his hand and looked me in the eyes.

"There is something about you, Mary Kaye," he said, gently wiping tears from my face. "I love you, and these young cats out here are not going to appreciate the jewel that you are. This time I'm playing for keeps."

He told me he was looking for that one special queen that he could build an empire with. He told me I was always the one, and that no one could take my place in his heart. Jonathan and I got back together, and while things went well at first, it wasn't long before I started hearing rumors of him cheating with yet another girl. She was still in high school but spent most of her days working with him.

The girl he had with him most days was a seventeen-year-old named Jasmine. It wasn't abnormal for him to have a female working with him, so I wasn't suspicious when I first met her. Plus, she knew I was his girlfriend and that we were living together. However, while at the mall one day I ran into my sister and brother-in-law, and they warned me that Jonathan was near one of the exits sitting down with a girl on his lap.

When I checked things out, sure enough, it was Jasmine sitting on his lap with her arm around his shoulder. My heart dropped, and I quickly decided that I would not confront him out of fear that he would make a fool of me in front of his friends who were all crowded around him. When he came home that night, I asked him about Jasmine. "I saw you at the mall today."

"And?" he asked.

"And I saw Jasmine had her arm around you and sat on your lap."

"And?"

"Are you messing with her?"

"Leave me alone, Mary Kaye. I haven't had any stress all day, and I come home and have to deal with this?" He started toward the door, put on his shoes, and grabbed his car keys. "Damn, you really starting to get on my nerves, you know that?"

Without another word, he left the house for the rest of the night. I found myself feeling guilty! I had dinner ready for him, and he wouldn't even be there to enjoy it. I lost my appetite. For the rest of the night, I just cuddled up with my son and tried to stop the racing thoughts. I couldn't help but wonder if he had left the house to see her. Knowing him, he probably seized the opportunity to find a reason to be upset with me so that he could leave. Suddenly, a plan came to my mind that I thought was sure to work.

I quickly looked at his phone records and took note of the numbers that showed up the most on the phone bill. I planned to block the house number and ask for Jasmine when the person picked up. If I had the wrong number, I would check the next number on the list. My heart was pounding as the phone rang on the other end. One ring. Two rings. Three rings.

"Hello?" said the person on the other line.

"Hi, may I speak to Jasmine, please?" I said in my best telemarketer voice.

"Speaking."

My heart was racing a million miles per second. My hands were shaking so bad that I could barely hold on to the phone.

"Jasmine, this is Mary," I said. "Jonathan just left the house after I asked him something about you. Is something going on between you guys?"

"Well, first of all, Jonathan told me he's not messing with you anymore," she said with an attitude.

I could almost hear her neck rolling as she continued. "He said he is not claiming you because you let some dudes run a train on you."

"If that was the case, why am I living here with him?" I snapped back. "I've been here for a while now."

"You're at his house now?" she asked with surprise in her voice. "Are you there babysitting your son, or are you spending the night?"

What kind of question was that? Am I babysitting my son? I asked her what she meant.

"Jonathan said that you come there sometimes to spend time with the baby."

I laughed. "Jasmine, I live here. You are still in high school, and I don't have time to play around with no little girls. Are you messing around with Jonathan or not?"

"Yes, I am, and he just called me and told me he's on his way over here."

Click.

She hung up the phone. I panicked because I knew she would tell him I called her. He would figure out that I had her phone number and that I had broken one of the rules of using the house phone. I was scared of what he would say or do. I cried myself to sleep while watching the clock wind down. It was nearly midnight before I could finally drift off. When I woke up the next morning, Jonathan was already in the shower. I tried to make him breakfast, but he just made himself a protein shake without speaking to me. When he finished, he grabbed his keys and walked out.

After he left, I realized that he had taken the house phone with him. Wow. I needed to get away from this prison of an apartment. I refused to go back to being stuck in this place every day without a soul to talk to, so I thought of a plan. Jonathan had a drawer that he would fill with loose change. I started rolling up quarters, dimes, nickels, and even pennies. Soon, I had nearly fifty dollars saved up. I started saving the plastic bags from the grocery store, and when he would send me to the store for groceries, I would hide the bags under my shirt.

I would steal pricey filet mignon, T-bone, porterhouse, and NY strip steaks so he would not question why I never had change when I returned from the store. While shopping, I would place all my groceries in the bags and casually walk out of the store. I did this for several weeks until I had over five hundred dollars saved up.

"I have to go down to my mom's house to do community service for that old shoplifting charge," I told him. I was lying but determined to get out of that apartment with my son. "I'm going to stay there until I finish so that you won't have to drive me back and forth every day."

I took enough clothes to last me for a few weeks. I didn't have much to begin with, so it didn't take long for me to pack up my son's things and mine and get out of there. I still had my Dodge Shadow, but it needed lots of work, so I barely made it down to my mother's house, which was an hour away. My mom and I had patched things up, and it felt good to be back home.

After a few days, the transmission went. I made it out just in time. With the five hundred dollars I had saved, I bought a red 1995 Dodge Neon. It was clean, cute, and great on gas. I checked the classifieds in the local newspaper and followed up on a few prospects. Within a few days, I was working evenings at a doctor's office doing telemarketing work.

I was also offered an overnight weekend position as a night auditor at a local Ramada, which was walking distance from my mom's house. The opportunities kept rolling in. My sister and an older cousin were working at a big insurance company, and they urged me to apply. They told me that a new training class was going to start soon and that I should move quickly. I applied, and after a few days, they offered me a position in customer service. Thank God that I had stopped smoking weed because the drug test was nearly impossible to pass. They clipped a huge chunk of your hair from the middle of your head to test for any drugs in your system.

When it was all said and done, I had secured three jobs in less than a couple of weeks after leaving Jonathan's house. Doors were just flying open. For a while, I worked all three jobs until finally narrowing it down to just two. I was making over six hundred dollars a week after taxes and loving my new independence.

By this time, Jonathan figured out that I wasn't coming back anytime soon. To his credit, he would come by every day after work, but my busy schedule left him with a lot of time to get away with indiscretions. I figured he was enjoying his privacy, so it shocked me when he asked if I would come back to his place. Although the drive to work would be a long one, he insisted that it would just be temporary.

"Start looking for apartments closer to your job," he said. "It's time for our son to have his own room anyway."

It sounded like a great idea, especially because my mom had moved in two of my younger cousins.

So, I went back. As soon as I walked into the apartment, I noticed the kitchen table was broken and lying on the floor. I also noticed that there was a bin in the front closet filled with women's clothes, hair products, and a curling iron. My picture that once sat propped up next to the couch was out of the frame and ripped up on the floor in the middle of the living room. It looked like he literally kicked someone out moments before moving me back in.

"Who did this?" I asked, angrily pointing to my ripped-up photo on the carpet. "Whose clothes are those in the closet? And what happened to the table?!"

"See? You ain't been here two seconds and you already looking for stuff!" he responded. "Don't you think we been through enough headaches already?"

He walked right back out of the door while I stood there holding our son. Some things never change.

Chapter 17

Ride or Die

My mind was all over the place. Did I imagine things? Did he move someone in and out that fast? Was it Jasmine? Was it Treniece or Tynika? Or maybe it was someone entirely new. I went into the bathroom to freshen up. As soon as I looked into the mirror, I was staring at a photo pressed into the edge of the glass.

Three girls who looked to be no more than sixteen years old were in the picture with just their underwear on. They had their backs turned and were bent over, attempting a seductive look at the camera. I felt disgusted. I heard Jonathan's keys at the door. I didn't even bother to confront him anymore.

"Just so you know, JP and his girl had to crash her for a few days," he explained. "I told her to take her stuff, but she must have forgotten some of it."

Did he leave to clear his head to come up with an explanation for this? Was that the best he could come up with? He must have thought I was a fool. I suppose I was a fool for even stepping foot back into that place.

"And what about my picture?" I asked. "Who ripped it up?"

"I don't know, Mary Kaye. All I know is that you are the only stress I've had all day. Why is that? Can't I just get some peace and quiet? Sheesh!"

He stormed into the bedroom. I left my son to play with his Teletubby on the floor of the living room and followed him.

"Yo, leave me alone, Mary Kaye. If you want to argue, go back to your mom's house with that."

"I just wanted to come in here and lay down with you."

He gave me a mean look, bit his bottom lip, and brushed past me. He left the bedroom and went back into the living room. I followed him and sat next to him on the couch in silence.

He shook his head, said something under his breath, got up, went back to the bedroom, and closed the door. I finally got the point. After a few minutes, I went to the bedroom door and listened. He was laughing and talking on the phone. By the sound of his voice, I could tell it was a female. I decided to take a shower and get ready for bed. I needed to clear my mind. However, all the anger and hurt rose up in me once again when I saw my cute turquoise Gillette shaver sitting on the edge of the bathtub filled with some other chick's pubic hair. Ugh! What did I do to deserve this?

Whoever this mystery female was that he had moved in so quickly was determined to leave her mark behind. She even left her asthma medication in the bathroom closet. Maybe she thought she was coming right back? Maybe he was still dealing with her?

I went to work the next day in a daze. I was determined to make a good impression as a new hire, but I was distracted by all the drama back at home. Over the next few days, I would find things like panties under the sofa cushion, condom wrappers behind the couch, women's underwear in random drawers, and more naked pictures of young girls. I told myself that he would change if I just showed him that I could love him in spite of his mistakes. I wanted to prove to him that no matter what he had a ride or die chick.

Most of all, I wanted to win. I didn't want any of these females to think that I was going to give him up so easily.

So I cooked, cleaned, and took care of our son the best way I knew how. I stopped asking questions. I quit my weekend job and helped him hustle on the weekends again. I even started dressing sexier and wore lingerie in the bedroom. I was so eager to please him that when he asked me if I would let him bring another female home, I readily agreed to it. However, I was completely caught off guard when one day I came home to a female that looked to be about forty years old straddled across my bed.

Based on his track record, I was expecting someone much younger. She was slim, and kind of cute if you squinted your eyes. Regardless of her looks, I was completely turned off by the whole ordeal because it felt like two old people were molesting me. During sex, it was even difficult for him to stay hard.

"I must be too excited," he explained.

Um, no. It probably had something to do with the fact that he paid her with crack cocaine to participate in this mess of a ménage à trois. When we finished, or should I say, when we gave up, she went into the bathroom and smoked her earnings. Ugh! It was the first time I suspected that he too must have been smoking crack.

He had to be out of his mind to pick this old broad to come home with us. No one should feel the need to be paid to be with a chick like me — male or female. It was also the moment I realized I was definitely not a lesbian, bisexual, bi-curious, or anything that had anything to do with me and another female in the same bed.

I thought it would be the first and last time I would ever do something like that. Boy, was I way off.

I ignored every red flag imaginable when it came to Jonathan. I pretended not to smell another woman's vagina on his mustache when he kissed me. I mustered up enough courage not to cringe and pull away because the smell was so repulsive. I ignored the phone calls he would make while in the other room. I listened to the giggling and seductive talk but pretended not to care.

Jonathan had convinced me that I was on a mission to see who could wear down an O.G. like him. I was in this secret competition of who would get him to marry them first. I was still wearing my ring, but there was no talk of wedding plans. However, now and then Jonathan would remind me of the story of a man who went digging for gold.

"He dug and dug and dug," Jonathan would say. "Under the hot sun, with sweat dripping down his head, he dug for that gold. He dug for years and years."

"Finally, he got tired of digging, so he threw down his shovel and walked away. Another man just happened to be passing by. When he saw the abandoned shovel, he picked it up and started digging. Almost immediately, he struck gold! The moral of this story: don't let one of these chickenheads out here scoop me up and take what's yours."

He would always warn me that if I ever decided to walk away, that would be the very moment that he would change his ways.

"You took a chance on this O.G., Mary Kaye. After giving all your time and mind to this relationship, you're just going to walk away? Good things come to those who wait, not to those who hate. All these other chickens out here hating on you because you were the first girl to take a chance at fate."

What I hated was how every serious conversation somehow turned into a rap song. Sometimes the rap didn't even make sense, but he would flow with it anyway as long as it rhymed. Somehow, I stayed and tried to wait for him to change. I had invested too much time into this. I was ready to see a return on my investment.

As Junior grew older, we realized that we needed a bigger apartment. I started hunting for a new place for us and got lucky when a co-worker told me that the first-floor apartment where he lived was now vacant. The location was about fifteen minutes closer to my job than our current apartment, and only about forty-five minutes from my mother.

We checked it out and fell in love with it. The entire place was huge. Two bedrooms, dining room, and a large kitchen. There was also a decent sized backyard that had a pathway to the library behind us.

Maybe now things will change, I secretly thought.

After getting settled in and buying new furniture, I felt at home. I was still working at the insurance company and had received a pay increase. I had full benefits and could carry the rent on my own if necessary. The best part was that everything was in my name. I finally felt like an adult. Everything appeared to be going well, but then I got a message from my mom to call my grandmother. When I called her up, she answered the phone in her usual thick southern accent.

"Heyyy, this you, Mary Kaye?" my grandmother said from the other end of the phone call.

"Yes, Mommole," I said, calling her by the nickname all her grandchildren affectionately used.

"Your momma told you what I said?"

"No, ma'am. She just told me to call you right away."

"Well, you know I love ya, and I've been praying for ya. During prayer, I heard the Lord tell me to tell you that 'it's time to make a move.' I think you know what I'm talking about, right?"

"I think so."

"Chile, I'm telling you the truth. If you don't move on, things are going to get so much worse."

My immediate thought was that things could not get much worse than what they already were. Plus, things were finally starting to fall into place. Jonathan was taking me out on dates again, and even coming home some nights. I brushed off my grandmother's warning and tried not to let it worry me too much.

My grandmother's words would come back to haunt me just several weeks later. I was away in South Carolina for a funeral when I woke up on my grandmother's couch drenched in blood. I was having a miscarriage.

Chapter 18

Indecent Proposal

At first, I thought I was having a heavy period, but when I went to the bathroom to clean up, huge blood clots were coming out of me. All of sudden, I felt like an even bigger blood clot was coming down, so I caught it with the tissue I had in my hand. What I saw brought me to tears. I could see what was clearly a tiny fetus lying right there on the clump of tissue.

Although I had no idea that I was pregnant until the miscarriage, I was devastated because I desperately wanted to have another child with Jonathan. He always expressed his desire to have two children by the same female.

"The one that has two babies by me is the one I'm going to marry," he would say.

After recovering from the initial shock, I buried my baby in my grandmother's yard. I was too embarrassed to tell anyone that I had gotten pregnant, so I suffered in silence for that entire morning. I couldn't get the image of my baby's cute little hands, fingers, and feet out of my head. I would have never thought that something so tiny could look so human.

Later that day, I gathered enough courage to call Jonathan and break the news to him. For some reason, I felt extremely nervous about what his reaction might be. Sure enough, he was furious, but for all the wrong reasons.

"What?! A miscarriage? You playing games with me, Mary Kaye?"

"No, I'm not. It just happened this morning."

I was crying uncontrollably at this point. He had no compassion in his voice.

"You and Jasmine think y'all slick. Y'all playing games. Did you talk to her today?"

"Huh? What are you talking about?"

"She just called me a few minutes ago talking about she had a miscarriage too. Y'all trying to set me up or something?"

Wow. I hung up the phone and sat there for a few minutes trying to digest what I had just heard. He admitted to me in one conversation that he was still screwing Jasmine. Furthermore, we had miscarriages on the same day? It was too weird and too much to handle while being miles away from home. All I could think of was him and Jasmine playing house while I was away.

When I got back home, a giant teddy bear and chocolates sat in the corner on my side of the bed. I thought to myself, *He wants to make it up to me for being so mean while I was away.* However, that did not take away from the fact that he let it slip that he was still messing with Jasmine. Each time I tried to talk about the miscarriage and his dealings with Jasmine, he reminded me how much I had hurt him in the past.

"Ever since you cheated on me with that young scrub and had that abortion, you took a huge chunk of my löve for you out of my heart. You let this dude run a train on you, but I took you back. A nigga like me needs to feel powerful. You need to stop worrying about Jasmine and start thinking about how you gonna win my heart back."

After a few days of hearing him throw the situation with Tyrone in my face, and me fighting back the urge to tell him that Tyrone and his friend raped me, I became so worn down that I was just ready to let the whole thing go. I settled back into my routine of going to work, picking up our son, cooking dinner, and going to bed.

Weeks would go by without us being intimate with one another. However, I didn't mind. Every time I would lie down next to him at night images of him with another female raced through my head. It was a major turn off. When he came home one day telling me I need to get tested for Chlamydia, I didn't even flinch.

"All right. But who done burned you though? It wasn't me," I said.

"Jasmine told me I gave her Chlamydia. I don't have it, but apparently somebody gave it to her. It must have passed from you to her."

His logic was so ridiculous; I didn't even have the energy or the patience to argue. I was exhausted from his lies and manipulation. I hated how he always insulted my intelligence, but my pride would not let me walk away from this crazy relationship. I knew everyone was waiting for the relationship to end.

I decided to humor him and get tested by my ob-gyn. After testing negative, I asked my doctor to please write a note for my "fiancé" letting him know that there was no trace of any STD. I remember the look she gave me. It said something like, "If you need to go through all this, why are you with him?"

When I showed him the note from my doctor, Jonathan dismissed it and changed the subject. I dropped the entire issue because I did not want to face the fact that once again he revealed he was still cheating on me with Jasmine while I was playing housewife.

One day, I thought things were finally going to get better when Jonathan called me at work to tell me he wanted to take me out that night. "My sister is going to watch Junior for us tonight. I want to take you out to eat and spend some quality time with my baby."

That evening, he took me to a TGI Fridays and a movie. We laughed and talked all night — it felt like old times. When we pulled up at the house, he turned off the engine and sat for a few seconds.

"What is it?" I asked.

"I finally realized that I can't spend the rest of my life without you," he said. "When I look at our son, it makes me feel so powerful, but I want to get that same feeling when I look at you."

"The problem is that I can't seem to forget about you and this scrub. I need you to replace that image in my mind with something else. I figured out what might help me to get over that hurt."

I couldn't have possibly been ready for what he was about to say next.

"I need to feel like a king," he continued. "Jasmine has been having some issues with her parents because she's been spending so much time hustling with me. They want her out of the house. She knows we're together, but I realized we might be able to kill two birds with one stone. I need you to seriously consider letting Jasmine come live with us."

I looked at him as if he had lost his natural mind. He didn't miss a beat. "If you do this, Mary Kaye, you will make me feel like the most powerful man on this earth! To be able to have sex with both of y'all at the same time. This is what I need to get over you and that scrub."

It sounded so crazy, but yet, I was even crazier for entertaining this conversation! "I don't know, Jonathan," I said. "She doesn't have anywhere else to go?"

I couldn't believe I was talking about this nonsense. However, at that point, I thought this would finally show him that I loved him, and I would do anything to make the relationship work.

"No, she doesn't have anywhere else to go. Think about it and let me know. Everything will be on your terms."

The next day, I went to work and couldn't think of anything else but his indecent proposal. He had a lot of nerve! Why was I even considering it? Would this finally let Jasmine know once and for all that I was the one who had his heart?

When Jonathan picked me up from work that night, I told him what my terms were.

"OK, I will think about it, but first Jasmine needs to get tested for any STDs. Don't think I forgot about that whole Chlamydia thing. Also, you can't have sex with her unless we're all together. If I say yes, it would only be for a few weeks, tops. Finally, she cannot bring her son."

The last part was crucial for me. My worst fear was that he would move her in and find every excuse to prolong her stay. I figured her son would be the thing that would make her leave sooner rather than later.

"OK, I'll let her know. I also told her that she's going to work at the strip club at night and bring some money into the house. Don't forget, you're the boss, Mary Kaye."

Jonathan was on cloud nine. However, by the time the next evening rolled around, I still hadn't given him a definitive answer. I was still contemplating everything when I heard his keys in the door. To my surprise, he walked in carrying two bags. He sat them on the living room floor with a huge grin on his face.

He went back out to the car, and when he returned the second time, Jasmine was with him, carrying the rest of her belongings. Instead of setting them down on the floor with her other two bags, she went straight to the bedroom without saying a word.

Chapter 19

Fool's Gold

Fury was rising inside me, and I could no longer hold back. I wanted to yell, "What the hell are you doing?! I told you I would think about it!"

But all that came out in a small voice was, "I thought you said I could think about it."

"Her dad made her get out tonight, Mary Kaye. What was I supposed to do?" he said. "I know you didn't want me going to a hotel room with her."

Jasmine walked back into the living room and sat down on my leather sofa. She glanced up at Jonathan with an impatient look and crossed her arms.

"Where do you want me to put the rest of my stuff?" she asked him.

There I was, the woman of the house, looking down at this girl sitting on my couch like she was in the VIP section waiting for someone to serve her. I needed her to understand her role from that point forward. I answered her question. "I'll clean out a couple of drawers for you," I said. "So, did you get tested?"

Jasmine gave me a confused look. Clearly, Jonathan never even asked her to get checked out for STDs.

"What are you talking about, Mary Kaye?" Jonathan intervened. "See, this is exactly what I be talking about with you. You always starting some mess. And you wonder why I'm out here looking for somebody real in the first place."

"Don't think I don't see what you up to. You're trying to make her leave," he continued, "and I'm going to end up leaving with her if you don't stop playing games. She's here now, so let's just have some fun. Damn! You're turning me off already!"

Ranting was Jonathan's tried and true method of fast-talking himself out of sticky situations and turning things around to the point where I would end up apologizing for a mess that he created.

The three of us ended up having sex that night for the first time. It was at least more enjoyable than the last time he tried to have a ménage à trois with me and that crackhead. However, I must admit that I was more concerned with showing Jasmine that I had no problem pleasing my man sexually.

After things were over, we all settled under the covers, with Jasmine in between the two of us. It was weird. I didn't like that she was here so suddenly. I didn't like how loud she yelled and moaned during sex. She had a high-pitched shriek that got on my last nerve. The thing that disgusted me the most was that she was still seventeen years old and in high school.

Somehow, I fell asleep. However, I woke up in the middle of the night from the sound of moaning. At first, I thought I was dreaming, but I was jolted out of my sleep when I rolled over and saw Jonathan on top of Jasmine. My heart was crushed. I was embarrassed by the tears that began flowing down my face. It was only the first night, and he was already breaking the rules I had set in place! I was devastated.

What hurts the most was that when Jonathan and I made eye contact, he gave me such a look of pity that he made me feel like an intruder in my own house. I rolled over and faced the wall. I silently cried until I finally fell asleep.

They continued this pattern for weeks. The weeks eventually turned into months and the months turned into a year and a half. In the meantime, Jasmine got pregnant again and gave birth to a baby boy. It became the norm to walk in on them having sex. I would get up to go to the bathroom in the middle of the night, open the bathroom door, and they'd be in there going at it. I would walk into the living room, and they would be on the couch screwing. My son even walked in on them one day.

It eventually got to the point where they would stay out for days at a time. I stopped having sex with Jonathan due to disinterest and disgust, and I no longer wanted to be a part of what they had going on. I had even started sleeping on the couch at night. It was obvious to me that he had no plans to send her back home to her parents, so I planned to let him get tired of her and eventually realize that I was a true ride or die chick.

I focused on paying my bills on time, saving my money, and building up my credit score. Jonathan and I had plans to get another vehicle, but this time it would be in my name. How could he plan a life with me if he wanted to keep Jasmine around? To me, this was a clue that regardless of his current actions, he wanted to be with me. Looking back at those times, I know now that it was foolish thinking.

When my credit score shot up, we were finally able to buy the car of our choice. We settled on a red GMC Denali. Jonathan was excited, and I was happy to give him something Jasmine was too young, inexperienced, and incapable of doing at that time. Plus, things were not so gravy between Jonathan and Jasmine after the baby arrived. She started begging him to let her older son come to the house from time to time. When he refused, she realized he cared less about her than she initially believed.

"Can he just visit for one day?" she pleaded.

"Leave me alone about your son, Jasmine. You already know you're not supposed to be here in the first place," he would say. "You want to be with your son? Go ahead and leave."

I could tell she was starting to see his true colors. Secretly, I enjoyed seeing them argue. However, when it came to her absent son, I could relate to her as a mother, and I started to sympathize.

"If you want, I can take you to see your son one day," I told her. "Jonathan doesn't have to find out."

Soon after that conversation, she trusted me enough to take her to see her son. On the drive to her parents' house, we finally bonded in a way that we did not think was possible. We realized we had more in common than just Jonathan.

"I don't know how you put up with him sometimes," she said. "He would never talk to me the way he talks to you."

"I'm not worried about him. You just wait; one day you'll see the real Jonathan."

I knew my warning was falling on deaf ears. Soon enough, Jasmine would find out for herself just how cruel and controlling Jonathan could be. In fact, that day would arrive sooner rather than later.

One day, while I was preparing dinner, Jasmine and Jonathan had a huge argument that escalated quickly. She finally started to see the side of Jonathan that I had become accustomed to. When she stood up to him and raised her voice in anger, he flew off the handle and became enraged.

"Who do you think you're talking to, Jasmine?" he demanded. "Keep talking, and I'll snap your damn neck!"

Jasmine decided not to back down, and this infuriated him even more. Before I knew it, Jonathan had grabbed her by her throat and was choking her against the kitchen wall. As she gasped for air, I did my best to run to her rescue. I tried to grab Jonathan's arms, and I urged him to stop before he killed her. However, when I saw the fury in Jonathan's eyes, I knew it would be nearly impossible for me to pry his hands away from her neck.

"Let her go! Do you want to go to jail?" I screamed.

I knew the only thing that would resonate with him at this point would be the negative consequences of his actions. However, instead of letting her go, he flung Jasmine across the floor like a rag doll and pulled her into the bedroom. He threw her on the bed, turned around, and slammed the door behind him. As soon as I heard him leave out of the front door, I ran to Jasmine to see if she was all right.

"You said you would never hit me!" Jasmine screamed through tears. "You promised you would never hit me!"

Jonathan was already gone, but I just let her release her pain and anger. I tried to calm her as I inspected the bruises on her neck, but she brushed me off. I knew she was upset at how I handled it.

"I only asked him if he wanted to go to jail because I knew that would make him stop," I explained.

She wiped her face as tears continued to stream down her cheeks. "Whatever," she said. "I don't care."

I decided that there was nothing more I could do to help at this point. Jonathan had put his hands on me on several occasions, but I never shared the incident with anyone because I didn't want to look even more foolish for staying with him all these years. I wanted to share that with her, but I kept silent and just stayed close by in case she needed me. However, I was relieved that Jonathan had left the house, because it meant I could have some peace and quiet for a short while. My son and I ate dinner, and after watching a movie, I fell asleep on the couch.

Surprisingly, Jasmine and I became even closer after this incident. She began confiding in me and telling me more about what they were up to when they would stay out all night. She told me how Jonathan would take her to adult stores and have her pick out women for him. Apparently, they had frequent threesomes with a random woman of her choosing. The horrifying part of it all was that she claimed he never used condoms with these strangers.

"You mean he had sex with all these women raw? Random women?"

"Yup, sometimes we'll be in the grocery store, at the gas station, or at the mall and he'll point someone out and ask for my permission to have sex with them."

I could not believe what I was hearing! Then again, I had to admit that if he was having all of these babies on the side, he had to have had plenty of unprotected sex in the past. At that point, I was grateful that I was avoiding sex with him. However, I still felt betrayed. Here he was, living with two women and that still wasn't enough for him. Why should I continue to put up with this nonsense? My mind kept thinking back to his story about the man digging for gold. Was I digging for fool's gold? Was I hoping that this man would change for the sake of our relationship, or was I just hoping to prove everyone wrong?

Whatever the case might be, I knew something had to give. I was holding on to false hope. Jonathan would never change, and the longer I allowed him to manipulate me, the more pain I would have to go through. I was hurt, embarrassed, and angry all at the same time.

Chapter 20

The Long Con

One day, Jasmine confessed that she and Jonathan had a long-term plan to con me into putting the Denali in my name and then they would both move out and leave me at the apartment. He told her to start befriending me and gain my trust long enough for me to put my guard down. They secretly plotted to push me to a point where I no longer wanted him, and they could be together once and for all. When she told me all of this, I felt like my world had crumbled. How could I not see this coming?

Suddenly, my rage turned from Jonathan to Jasmine. She was in my house, and how dare she think she was going to come up in here thinking some freakiness in the bedroom was going to trump everything I had to offer Jonathan! My young mind was still trying to fight for this tragedy of a relationship.

"What I don't understand is why he feels the need to cheat on me?" I said.

"You don't really know Jonathan," she tried to explain. "He likes to do some freaky stuff, and he said he doesn't feel comfortable letting you see that side of him."

"What? Like the fact that he likes to wear women's panties during sex?" I said with a smirk on my face.

She gasped and jumped back like I had slapped her in the face. "How do you know that?!" she exclaimed with her hands covering her mouth, and her eyes stretched wide in disbelief. "He said he couldn't tell you stuff like that."

"Trust me, I know all of his secret fantasies and his kinky side," I said. "He played you because I've known that for years and he's done it quite a few times."

When I told Jasmine some of the things he shared with me about her and her family secrets, she realized that Jonathan and I were closer than she had previously believed. I could see the disappointment and hurt in her facial expressions. Based on the things I shared, she began to understand that I wasn't the only one being deceived.

"You know what? I found out he's cheating with another chick named Desiree," she confessed. "He was staying at a hotel, and when I called the room, she answered the phone."

"I am not even surprised," I said. "I'm almost numb to his shenanigans."

"I bet he's there with her right now," said Jasmine. "While we up in here stuck in this house."

Out of nowhere, she burst into tears. "I never thought that he would cheat on me. Now I feel like a home-wrecker!" she cried.

Oddly enough, I felt her pain. She thought she was going to have a shot at turning this player into a prince, and in that regard, we shared the same young and dumb sentiments. On the other hand, I resented her for coming into my home and interrupting what I thought was a new and improved life for Jonathan and me. We cried together for what seemed like hours.

Jasmine admitted that she felt like a prisoner in our house, and how she wanted to go out with her friends sometimes, but Jonathan would always come up with some excuse as to why she could not go. She didn't know how to drive yet, and Jonathan would not teach her. To make matters worse, we were both so far away from our families that it was nearly impossible for her to take public transportation.

"If you want to go somewhere on the weekends, I'll take you," I told her. When I saw the relief and excitement in her eyes, I took things one step further. "I can teach you how to drive too!"

"Really? I can't wait to get my license. I'm getting sick of depending on everybody else for rides."

Over the course of the next few weeks, we went to the mall, we had lunch, and we had long chats about everything from fashion, our families, our children, and everything else in between. She told me about her dreams for the future, and how she regretted dropping out of high school to run behind Jonathan. I confessed that I was battling anxiety and depression and how my doctor had given me a prescription to help me cope.

"See! My doctor gave me a sample of Zoloft, but I only took it for a few days," I said. "I don't like how jittery it makes me feel."

"Does Jonathan know about it? Does he even care about how you've been feeling?" she asked.

"Nope. And I don't want him to know. Sometimes I feel like I'm losing my mind," I told her. "If I didn't have Junior, I would have probably killed myself a long time ago."

"Why? You just have to learn how to stand up to him. He treats you like that because no matter what he does, you still stick around."

The nerve! How dare she question my inability to defy him when he had tossed her around like a rag doll not too long ago! She was in another woman's house, away from her son and family, all because she wanted to take my man and claim him for herself. In hindsight, we were both stupid, and she was just eighteen-years-old at the time. Furthermore, I had been with this forty-three-year-old man since I was fifteen. Our young minds could not comprehend the severity of the situation.

"I have been with this man for years," I told her. "I might not have the perfect relationship, but I have my own place, we drive nice cars, we eat good, and my son gets to live with his dad — that's something I never had growing up."

"If I have to suffer for a season to give my son a good life, then that's what I am going to do." I was confident that I was making the best choice.

Furthermore, I knew what she was up to. Jasmine was just trying to discourage me and make me leave so that she could put up a front to her family and act like Jonathan was her man, and this was her house all along. I resented her even more, but somehow, I still had sympathy for her. However, things started getting very strange around the house. One day, Jasmine asked if she could use my flat iron. When she finished using it, I noticed she had styled her hair just like mine! When we went to the mall, she picked out the same outfits that I already owned.

When I asked her about it, she replied, "I just like the way you dress, and I didn't know what else to get."

However, it didn't stop there. She bought the same pink snow boots, DKNY outfits, and the same style of sunglasses I owned. After I told her I was thinking about having a birthday party for my mother and gave her all the intricate details, I found a list that she wrote out planning a similar party for her mom. When I told her that I considered going to school for culinary arts, I later found an application for a culinary arts school partially filled out by Jasmine. Ugh!

When I described a tattoo that I wanted, she later told me about her idea for a tattoo that was eerily similar to the one I had told her about — as if she completely forgot where she had gotten the idea! The situation was starting to get under my skin. In fact, it was downright annoying!

I strongly felt it was time to make some adjustments. Maybe the sooner I taught her how to drive, the sooner she would decide to go back to her parents' house. Plus, Jonathan and I were on good terms. He had not caught on to the fact that Jasmine and I were opening up to each other and hanging out on the weekends. He was too busy with his hustle and whatever new females he was out there pursuing. I started getting used to the life we had. My son was in daycare and doing very well, and I was working full time. I had my own car to come and go as I pleased, and I always had money in my pocket.

The best part was that I had enrolled back in school, but this time the degree program was online. On the home front, Jonathan was starting to lose interest in Jasmine. She was no longer a little girl with a tiny waistline and big butt. Motherhood had changed her body, stretch marks had set in, and her face was always stressed and tear-streaked. Clumps of tissues cluttered the nightstand from her frequent bouts of tears and sniffling. The only times Jonathan and Jasmine seemed to bond was when he would come home with weed.

I had long given up smoking weed, so they would shut the door of the bedroom and smoke because I didn't want my son to smell it, nor did I want it all through the house. What upset me about their habits was that they would always have their baby in the room with them. When I confronted both of them about it, Jasmine gave me a look of annoyance and rolled her eyes.

"Weed isn't going to hurt the baby. You always think you know everything, Mary Kaye," said Jonathan. "Why don't you mind your business?"

I no longer felt the sting of his words when he would snap at me. I just shrugged it off and went on about my business. He started to notice my nonchalance when dealing with him and commented on it. "I raised you from a quiet, little girl and groomed you into a powerful lady," he would say.

He said stuff like this from time to time with all sincerity, as if it were perfectly normal. It would be funny if it weren't so tragic.

I felt everything but empowered by this relationship. In fact, I felt trapped and lonely. As bad as it was, I was determined to prove everyone wrong, and beat Jasmine at this "game."

Chapter 21

She's Going To Take Your Spot

One day, Jonathan confided in me that he felt he made a huge mistake by bringing Jasmine into our lives. "I wish I had never done that to you. Her father warned me about her too — she's lazy. She doesn't work, she doesn't know how to cook, she's sloppy, and doesn't clean up behind herself," he would say. "She's nasty. Look at all these tissues on the dresser and the floor. She leaves her dirty panties all over the place. She's such a turnoff!"

"Well, you brought her here, so why don't you just tell her to leave?" I asked.

"You can't just kick somebody out," he said. "That's against the law. Plus, her father told me not to bring her back."

"Don't worry. When she sees us shining together, she's not going to want to stick around," he said. "Give me another son, Bootie. If you do that, I'll feel like the most powerful man on earth."

He went through the same tired speech about how he dreamed of having two children with the same woman, and how he would likely marry the woman that would accomplish this great "feat."

"Jasmine is going to get pregnant again, just watch," he warned as if she would magically conceive by herself. "You let this chick get pregnant, and she's going to think she can take your spot."

Instead of seeing through this twisted logic, I fed right into it. I immediately set my sights on getting pregnant as soon as possible. When pregnancy test after pregnancy test kept turning up negative, I started to panic. I wasn't on birth control, and even though sex was few and far between, I had no problems getting pregnant in the past.

A few months went by, and I still wasn't pregnant. A year had passed since I stopped taking birth control, so I started wondering if I was infertile. It seemed unlikely at my age, but I wasn't sure, so I made an appointment to see Dr. Klineman, my ob-gyn. After running a few tests, Dr. Klineman called me back into her office to discuss an unusual discovery.

"When you gave birth to your son, did the OP report say anything about your tubes and ovaries being deformed?" she asked.

The OP report was the operative report that was recorded after having my C-section.

"Not that I recall. Why do you ask?"

"Your OP report says that you have two normal, healthy fallopian tubes and ovaries," Dr. Klineman explained. "However, your results are showing that you have just one tube and one ovary. In fact, where there used to be an additional tube and ovary, I see a remnant of what used to be there. It's like they disintegrated."

I was shocked! A million questions raced through my mind as I wondered what this meant. Did this mean I wouldn't be able to have any more children? When did this happen? How did it happen?

"I wouldn't worry too much," Dr. Klineman reassured me. "The body has a way of compensating for what is missing. However, it may take longer to get pregnant because you will only ovulate every other month," she explained.

My newly discovered health issue would drastically lessen my chances of getting pregnant before Jasmine! I had to do something. I was so determined to get pregnant that I scheduled an appointment with a fertility clinic. Meanwhile, I requested a copy of my OP report from my C-section.

What I read in the report puzzled me even more. The report did in fact state that I had normal tubes and ovaries. What happened in the last few years that caused me to lose a tube and ovary? Was it the abortions? Did the surgeon accidentally sever my reproductive organs during the C-section and lie to cover it up?

Whatever the case was, it was going to be nearly impossible to figure out what happened at this point. My main concern now was to get pregnant as quickly as possible so I could move on with my life without Jasmine being a part of it. Although we shared friendly conversations from time to time, she seemed to be obsessed with me by wearing the same clothes, hairstyles, and even trying to talk like me. I decided to distance myself because it was starting to get a bit awkward, but I promised her I would teach her how to drive.

"It's nice out today," I said. "We can go out to the parking lot and practice driving if you want. Plus, we might as well do it now before something happens to the car."

We got the kids dressed and packed up the car. I put the key in the ignition and turned. Nothing.

"Maybe it's the battery," said Jasmine.

"I have no idea. It could even be the starter," I said while trying to crank the engine a few more times.

Neither of us knew what we were talking about. The only thing we knew for certain was that we were not going anywhere today. We walked back into the house disappointed.

"Wow, and you just said something might happen to the car too," Jasmine said.

When she put her things away, she shut the bedroom door and watched television with her son for the rest of the day until Jonathan came home that night. When he came home, I was sitting in my normal spot in the living room. He walked past me with only a few words and made his way to the bedroom where Jasmine was waiting. For the first time in a while, I felt stuck all over again.

I had a feeling Jonathan would take his time getting the car fixed as a means to keep me in the house more. Sure enough, when he came out of the bedroom long enough to eat the dinner I had prepared, he fussed about the car until finally concluding that I would pay for it myself. "I don't know what you did to that car, but I'm not getting it towed, and you're going to pay for it to be fixed."

"What about the rent? Are you going to cover it this month?" I asked.

We alternated months paying the rent, and it was my turn to pay. My account had been recently depleted from my weekend trips to the shopping mall with Jasmine. Plus, I had just bought my computer for my online classes.

"No, I'm not paying for shit! You knew something was going to happen to that car," he said. "I don't know what you did to it, but Jasmine told me you did something."

"Huh?" Did I just hear him correctly?

"Yeah, you didn't think she would tell me, did you? She told me how you trying to be all up in her face," said Jonathan. "You trying to act like you want to teach her to drive, and then got the nerve to tell her something was going to happen to the car. You knew you had done something to that car all along, Mary Kaye."

My mouth dropped open. I was so confused, hurt, and angry all at the same time. How could she betray me like this? I thought she wanted to keep things quiet to avoid him interfering with her learning to drive. Yet, he knew all along! Why would she tell him that I did something to the car when I was only trying to help her? I looked at her, but she was busy eating a plate of food that *I* had prepared. The nerve!

"Oh, you thought she was your friend? Aww. She told me how you take depression medication, too," he said. He started laughing that dumb laugh of his. "You stupid, Mary Kaye. Keep taking those white man drugs if you want to!"

Jasmine was still eating, avoiding eye contact. I wanted to slap the plate out of her hand. I was moments away from snatching her up when she stood up and walked towards the kitchen to put her plate in the sink. As she brushed past us, she mumbled something under her breath.

"What did you say?" I asked as she walked by.

"You knew what was going to happen to that car before we even got in it," she said.

She wouldn't even look back at me as she put her plate in the sink and walked away.

"What sense does that even make, Jasmine? I'm trying to help you out. How am I going to get to work now?"

Jonathan snickered through this entire exchange.

"How you let her fool you like that? You should've known Jasmine was not your friend," he laughed.

I hated the both of them. I was sick of his nonsense, and I was sick of my on-again, off-again friendship with Jasmine. I felt like she was only using me to get what she needed and just wanted to become more like me. We stopped talking to each other from that day forward.

The more Jonathan and Jasmine smoked weed together, the sillier they got around the house. They bonded even more by getting high every day, and I started to feel like a stranger in my own house. The resentment was starting to be too much. I found the half filled out application for culinary arts school and saw that Jasmine had included her social security number and birthdate.

What I did next was out of pure hatred and revenge. I created a fake BlackPlanet account and posted her personal information for the world to see. I even posted her mom's address. Next, I took her state identification card and threw it out the window. However, I still wasn't satisfied. I needed some immediate gratification.

Chapter 22

Sweet Revenge

Jasmine liked using body washes and hairspray a lot and had an almost full bottle of body wash in the shower. I spit into both bottles multiple times, but that just didn't seem devious enough. I pondered for a moment before coming up with a brilliant idea.

One morning after taking a shower, Jasmine rushed out of the bathroom holding her hairspray in the air. She went straight to Jonathan and asked him to smell her hair and then smell the contents of the bottle. I watched in amusement as I innocently prepared breakfast, but I knew shit was about to hit the fan.

"What does this smell like to you?" she asked him.

"I don't know; it smells kind of funny," he said. "What is it supposed to smell like?"

"It's not supposed to smell like this," said Jasmine.

She stormed into the kitchen where I was standing and asked the million-dollar question.

"Did you piss in my hairspray?"

It took everything for me not to laugh in her face. However, I kept my composure, and with a straight face I replied, "Nope."

"You liar!"

"Did you spray some of that on your hair?" Jonathan asked her with amusement all over his face.

"Yes!"

With that, I just couldn't hold back anymore. Apparently, neither could Jonathan because before I knew it, we were both in tears laughing.

"You might want to throw out your body wash too!" I said through fits of laughter.

It was the first time in a long time that Jonathan and I laughed together like that. Not only that, but it felt good that it was at Jasmine's expense. After we calmed down, Jonathan demanded that I buy her another bottle of hairspray and body wash.

"I have to admit, that was classic," he said, still chuckling. "I can't wait to tell everybody what you did."

Needless to say, Jasmine and I could no longer even fake a friendship after that incident. Things got even tenser after I shared some good news.

"I'm preggnaaant!" I yelled in a sing-song type of way from the bathroom.

To throw it in Jasmine's face even more, I bought books on pregnancy and strategically placed them around the house. My goal was to keep reminding her that I was not only the woman of the house, but that I was expecting Jonathan's second child as well. I knew she understood exactly what this meant.

I was on cloud nine. Every day felt great. I went to work, came home, and Jonathan catered to me as if I were the Queen of Sheba. I cooked, cleaned, and paid bills while Jasmine sat around the house all day and watched television in between her son's temper tantrums. I got through my first set of classes with straight A's, and Jonathan got my car fixed to avoid having to drive me back and forth to my prenatal visits.

When I was about five months pregnant, Jonathan took Junior and me to see the UniverSoul Circus one Sunday evening. We met his sister there and enjoyed the night as one big happy family. When we came home that night, Jasmine was sitting in the living room with a depressed look on her face. I took one look at her and could tell she had been crying for hours. We were still laughing and talking about the night as if she didn't exist. She walked up to Jonathan and demanded that he take her home that very second.

"My friend Tasha saw y'all at the circus and told my sister," said Jasmine. "Now my parents know Mary Kaye is pregnant, and that y'all still together! You got me up here looking stupid!"

"You want to leave, Jasmine? All right! Let Mary Kaye win," he spewed. "Go ahead, get your shit and let's go. You just let her win!"

Jasmine already had her things packed, so they left the house in a matter of minutes, arguing the entire time. I sat up waiting for him to return. To my disappointment, they both walked back into the house around two o'clock in the morning. It was like déjà vu from the night she first arrived. They walked to the bedroom in silence. I didn't even bother getting into my own bed.

Here I was, five months pregnant and sleeping on the couch. It was impossible to sleep that night with the sounds of them having makeup sex booming all the way from the back of the house. With only a few hours until daybreak, I watched a few episodes of my favorite HBO series, "The Sopranos," until it was time to get ready for work.

I was so stressed that I started having early labor pains. My sixth month was brutal. I was in so much pain and under so much anxiety that I could barely make it through a day at work. I asked my doctor if she could write me a note stating that I needed to be on bed rest for a while. For some odd reason, she refused. I was miserable.

One day while at work taking customer calls, I had a huge urge to go to the bathroom. I tried to hold it and finish the call until I couldn't hold it any longer. I put the caller on hold and rushed to the restroom. After half-walking and half-running a few feet down the hallway, water gushed between my legs and soaked my tan cargo pants.

I looked down at my legs in horror. A co-worker saw me standing there in shock and realized what had happened. Someone quickly grabbed a chair and sat me down as I began to hyperventilate slightly. I was only twenty-seven weeks pregnant, and all I could think was how on earth could my baby survive if he was born now?

After a little over twenty-four hours in the hospital, I gave birth to a two-pound six-ounce baby boy. He was so tiny that I was afraid to touch him. I knew he would survive, but what I did not know was that the days ahead would be extremely tough. A few days after birth, he developed jaundice and the doctors placed him on medication for his kidneys and lungs. The doctors warned me of the potential complications that my baby could face, and soon enough my fears came to life.

The doctors explained that my baby was experiencing a brain stroke. In other words, the stress of childbirth caused his brain to start bleeding. Bleedings are graded from one to four, and his was a grade three bordering on four. I was terrified at what this could mean. The nurses in the pediatric ICU tried to reassure me that they see premature babies survive all the time and that soon I would have a healthy baby bigger than my first child, who was born full-term.

Although I did not have a strong relationship with God at the time, I began to pray more than I had ever prayed before. My mother insisted that I pray over my son every day. The doctors told me there was nothing they could do except wait for the bleeding to stop. He was too tiny for them to perform surgery, so we just waited. The bleeding eventually stopped but started clotting. The clotting blocked his left ventricle and started a domino effect of medical issues.

The blocked ventricle caused his spinal fluid to stay in his brain rather than flowing back to the spine. The fluid on his brain was then causing his brain to swell. I watched as my baby silently suffered through this crisis. He was so innocent and oblivious to all that was going on. Somehow, I knew he would be OK.

However, Jonathan had a more depressing outlook. He rarely came to visit because he claimed he did not want to get too attached in case our baby died. The doctors were not sure if he would survive and were also unsure if he would be able to walk, talk, or have a normal life even if he did pull through. Through all the negativity, I held on to hope.

Prayer and family support got me through one of the most difficult times of my life. I tried hard not to care about what Jonathan and Jasmine were likely doing back at home. I couldn't help but think they were pretending to have a carefree life, and that she was probably enjoying time with him — finally having him all to herself. But, my main concern was not at home. Junior and I stayed at the hospital night after night and spent our days near the tiny incubator where my tiny newborn slept.

After several months, it was time to come home. There would be lots of follow-up visits with neurologists, neurosurgeons, pulmonologists, and many other specialists in the days ahead. As I wrapped my baby tightly in his blanket and prepared him to come home for the first time, I realized that Jonathan never brought his car seat out of the car.

"We can't leave without him being in his car seat," I explained to Jonathan.

"I'm not going back outside to get that thing; just carry him downstairs."

"No, that's not how it works. The hospital has a policy where we have to have him in the car seat. They need to see that we actually have one and that we know how to use it."

"Why do you always have to listen to them crackers, Mary Kaye? I don't have to prove anything to them! They just want to make things extra difficult!"

Jonathan became louder, and the more I insisted that he follow the rules, the angrier he got. By this time, our son was wide awake, and Jonathan's aggressive behavior was starting to concern the nurses.

"I need to get back to work, and I don't have time to go all the way back downstairs to get that fucking car seat! You want to get the car seat? Go get it your damn self!"

"Our son is getting released from the hospital, and you're worried about getting back on the bus to hustle?"

I was surprised at my words. I was usually too afraid to challenge him. With fire in his eyes and his teeth clenched together, he got so close to my face that I thought he was going to choke me in front of the hospital staff.

"I'm about to leave your ass up here if you don't get your shit and come on," he said with spit flying from his mouth.

At this point, I couldn't hold back the tears anymore. I was so embarrassed.

"Why are you making a scene, Mary Kaye? Damn! It ain't that serious. I swear I'm about to leave your sorry ass up here! I'm taking my son and getting the fuck outta here!"

The nurses rushed over to make sure I was OK. They explained to Jonathan that he had to get the car seat out of the car and bring it to the pediatric ICU based on hospital rules and to make sure the car seat was safe to use. What I did not realize was that the nurses had also contacted the Department of Children and Families, a Social Services agency, out of concern for our child's safety.

None of us were sure what Jonathan was capable of doing at this point. He was yelling at me, at the hospital staff, and seemed seconds away from snapping. Our son was finally coming home, and this should have been a happy occasion. Instead, I was getting cursed out and threatened. Finally, the nurses offered to take the baby back into the room so that I could go downstairs and get the car seat myself.

When I got to the car, I realized the real reason Jonathan was in such a rush. It had nothing to do with getting back to work. Jasmine was in the car with not only Junior and her baby boy, but also with her older son, who had been living with her parents this entire time as well! It was all too much to process. Where were they going? Were they all coming home with us on the first day my son would be home? Not to mention the fact that she was in the front seat of the car! Where was I supposed to sit?

Without saying a word to her, I got the car seat and went back upstairs to the pediatric ICU. While wiping tears from my face, I let the nurses inspect the car seat and help me place my son comfortably inside. Jonathan was waiting outside the ICU entrance, talking on his cellphone. I could see that he was smiling and laughing. I suppose his impatience only kicked in when he was talking to me.

One of the nurses motioned for him to come back inside so that we could sign the discharge paperwork. She also explained that we had to wait for the transport assistant to bring a wheelchair for us. When Jonathan heard this, he went into another fit of rage.

"Hold up! You mean to tell me we been up here all this time, and you guys knew we had to have a wheelchair in order to leave?" Jonathan started pacing back and forth, shaking his head.

"What kind of hospital is this?!" he asked, throwing his hands up in frustration. "We not waiting for no wheelchair! You can call the cops if you need to, but we're leaving."

Jonathan grabbed the car seat by the handle and started walking towards the elevators. I had no choice but to follow him. I was not letting him take my baby anywhere without me! The nurses called security, but by the time they caught up to us, we were near the front exit of the hospital. The security guard was a young black male who looked to be in his late twenties. He immediately recognized Jonathan from hustling on the city buses, and his body language quickly changed from authoritative to apologetic.

"Yo, man, I apologize, but it's hospital rules," said the security guard. "You good, though."

"These crackers got it designed so that we have to do everything exactly the way they want it," Jonathan told the security guard. "Then they send another brother to come confront me to enforce *their* rules."

The security guard nodded his head in silent agreement. "I don't understand it either, man, but hey, don't worry. Just get home safe. Congratulations, by the way."

Jonathan always had the gift of gab and could talk his way out of any situation. With all that had just taken place, I realized we could have left a long time ago if he had just complied with the rules. However, somehow Jonathan was still upset with me. He refused to talk to me on the way to the car, and he didn't bother asking Jasmine to get out of the front seat. I silently settled into the backseat while fighting back angry tears.

I wanted to be close to my sons anyway. Jasmine's son, Rasheed, moved to the rear of the SUV with Jasmine's other son. I felt sandwiched in with Jonathan and Jasmine in the front, and her two sons behind me. My two sons and I sat in the middle. The circumstances seemed surreal. I was sitting behind my fiancé and his mistress, while they laughed and talked the entire way home.

Chapter 23

You're Nothing But a Sex Toy

During the ride home, Jonathan and Jasmine laughed and talked as if they were the only people in the car. What I gathered from their conversation was that she had a doctor's appointment to go to. The stopover at the hospital to pick up me and my son, who had been in the hospital for nearly three months, had made her late. After driving forty-five minutes back to the house, Jonathan helped me unload the baby's things and got us settled into the house. It was the least he could do. Jasmine stayed outside with her boys.

When I stepped into the living room, I was pleasantly surprised that Jonathan had put together a bassinet for our son. However, my smile quickly faded when reality set in. I had forgotten that the living room had become my bedroom. I had forgotten that I no longer slept in the bed with the father of my children, but that someone else had taken that place.

Jonathan and Jasmine left shortly after. I went to the bedroom to see what changes, if any, had taken place. I immediately noticed that Jasmine had taken over most of the bedroom, and her older son's clothes were neatly folded in one of the drawers. I asked myself how long he had been spending the night here without me even knowing?

When I glanced at the odds and ends sitting on the side of the bed, I noticed a bottle of prenatal vitamins. My antennas went up. On the floor next to the bed was one of my books about the stages of pregnancy. Hmm. With my hands shaking, I opened the top drawer on the side of the bed. Among the contents of the drawer was an ultrasound photo. I lost it.

I began grabbing at everything in the drawer, pulling the contents out and throwing them across the room. I knocked over Jasmine's toiletries, ripped up the ultrasound picture, ripped up the library book about pregnancy with no concern as to how I was going to explain this mess. I was grateful that both my sons were asleep in the living room. It gave me time to cry and release the pent-up anger I had been holding on to for months.

I didn't even bother cleaning up the bedroom after throwing my tantrum. When Jonathan and Jasmine returned with the kids, I was sitting on the couch feeding my baby as if nothing had happened. Without a word, I watched them make their way through the house and to the bedroom. I could hear Jasmine reacting to the mess I left for her. As Jonathan stormed to the front of the house where I was sitting, I prepared myself to get cussed out.

To my surprise, Jonathan just walked past me and out of the front door without saying a word. I heard him start the car and speed off. By now, my son had finished his tiny bottle of breast milk, so I settled him into his bassinet. As he lay sleeping, I cuddled up under a blanket on the couch in the hopes of getting some much-needed sleep as well. Before I could close my eyes and get comfortable, I was startled by the sound of Jasmine's son Rasheen running into the dining room bouncing a basketball.

Rasheen repeatedly threw the ball against the dining room wall, while Junior sat on the floor playing with one of his noisy LeapFrog games. I quietly motioned for them to keep the noise down because the baby was sleeping. Junior immediately understood and went into his room to play quietly. Rasheen ran into the kitchen where his mom was fixing a plate of spaghetti and started crying loudly.

"Stop that crying!" she yelled.

At this point, her baby, who was sitting in a car seat on the kitchen floor, also started screaming at the top of his lungs. Rasheen ran away from her and back into the dining room. He bounced the ball loudly in defiance.

"What did I tell you to do?" she yelled again. "You want me to give you a beating?"

She grabbed a belt and awkwardly swung it at him and missed. It was obvious she wasn't used to disciplining a child.

As amusing as this attempt at motherhood was, I had seen and heard enough. I got up from the couch and asked her if they could all keep the noise down because the baby was asleep.

She sucked her teeth. "Ain't nobody thinking about you," she sneered. "Take your dumb ass back in the living room."

My anger went from zero to one hundred! Did I miss the memo where this became her house and not mine? And why was her son here in the first place?!

"Who the fuck do you think you're talking to? This is my house; or did you forget?"

I was just getting started. "You ain't nothing but a sex toy, Jasmine," I continued. "The only reason you're here is because I let Jonathan bring you here."

By this time, she had gone back into the bedroom and sat on the edge of the bed with her plate of spaghetti. I followed behind her, spewing every word, hoping something I said would cut her deep. "You home-wrecker! You ain't nothing but a ho," I screamed into her face.

It infuriated me even more that she was calmly sitting there eating her food like this was her house. Her baby was sitting in his car seat at her feet, and Rasheen was still running through the house as if nothing was out of the ordinary.

"And tell your son to stop running through my house. He probably doesn't listen to you because he forgot you were even his mother! What kind of mother leaves her son behind to go live with her boyfriend and his fiancé?"

My final statement must have struck a nerve because she took the hot plate of spaghetti she was eating and flung it at me. I moved out of the way just in time, and the entire plate of hot food landed directly on top of her baby, who was propped up in his car seat. He screamed out in pain. I looked to see if the baby was OK, but before I knew it, Jasmine grabbed me by my hair.

We became tangled as we scratched at each other's faces, pulled each other's hair, and punched and kicked while our children cried in the background. When we finally separated from each other, I grabbed an iron off the dresser and swung at her face. When she saw that I was ready to do some serious damage, she grabbed her son and tried to leave the house. The fork she had been eating with was lying on the floor, so I quickly grabbed it and stabbed it deep into the back of her head until it stuck in.

Jasmine looked back at me with a shocked look on her face and tried to reach behind her head to see what she had stuck in the base of her skull. When she realized she couldn't pull it out, she ran to the back door with Rasheen at her side. When I saw that she was trying to leave without her baby, I grabbed him from the car seat. As she was going out the door, I thrust him into her arms and slammed the door behind them.

Jasmine ran to a neighbor's house and called the police. By the time the cops arrived to arrest me, Jonathan had come back home. Apparently, she called him too. In fact, he went to see her and her kids before coming into our house to check on us. The police charged me with risk of injury to a minor and assault with a weapon on a pregnant woman. The latter charge was an automatic felony.

The next time I saw Jasmine was in court because she had also been charged with risk of injury to a minor. We both had ugly scars covering our faces from all the scratching and ripping at each other. It was a shame that out of everything that happened, we were the ones who suffered the most. Jonathan was still hanging out and having fun with whatever female he chose for that week or month.

The only good thing that came out of that fight was that Jasmine was finally out of the house. She was forced to leave because she was not on the lease agreement, and the police would not allow us to remain at the same residence. Her family finally knew the truth. My family finally knew the truth. However, I think they knew all along or at least suspected. It was embarrassing, to say the least.

It felt good to have my house back to myself, though. Jonathan and I barely spoke in the weeks following, and I was good with that. I planned to work on getting my apartment as soon as possible. However, I knew if Jonathan caught wind of my plan, he would do his best to sabotage it. Plus, I didn't know what was going on with him and Jasmine — especially since she was expecting another child.

Eventually, my leave of absence ran out and I returned to work. My baby was getting stronger every day, and my mother started to watch him for me during the day. The support helped out a great deal. Reconnecting with my family gave me the confidence to leave Jonathan. I built up the courage to confide in my mom and told her that I wanted to leave him. I told her I would need to move my things out of the house while I looked for a new place.

My idea was to move without him realizing that I was packing up. Slowly but surely, I took bags of clothes to my mother's house, all while leaving just enough in our apartment so as not to arouse any suspicion. I told Jonathan I sold my computer so that he wouldn't think anything strange when he noticed it missing from its usual spot.

Jasmine left some of her clothes behind, so I used them as decoys in the closets and drawers while I moved out the last few items. My car had broken down again, and Jonathan was determined to keep me on a leash. He refused to have it fixed this time. However, I secretly rented a car on Fridays and Saturdays from Cheap Auto Rental and would park the car down the street from the house. Having a car allowed me to get back and forth from my mother's house as I slowly moved out.

On my lunch break at work, I checked out a cozy two-bedroom apartment that I saw advertised in the newspaper. It was a two-family house on a quiet street, and the place was perfect. I had no money for furniture, but income tax season was just around the corner. A few days later I put an eight hundred dollar deposit down, with a promise to pay the first and last month's rent on March 1.

It was 2005, and I was looking forward to finally being free from Jonathan. It had been seven years of manipulation, heartbreak, and hell, and I could finally see the light at the end of the tunnel. After being with this man all these years, I looked back on my life and realized that my childhood had passed me by. However, my new life was just beginning.

Chapter 24

Time to Let Go

One night I decided to go to a church service out of the blue. Jonathan kept me from anything remotely religious, so it had been ages since I stepped into a church. I was so proud of myself in a way; I knew it was only the grace of God that allowed me to escape from Jonathan.

After the service was over, the guest speaker approached me and asked if she could have a word with me.

"I could not let you leave without telling you what God has to say to you," she said. "He wanted me to tell you to let go. It might not seem like it right now, but you have a powerful voice inside of you. You are going to set an example for a lot of people, but before God can use you, you have to let go."

My eyes filled with tears, and she grabbed me and held me tight. It felt so genuine. I hadn't felt a sincere touch like that in a long time.

"You're hiding your depression, but I can see it. But, I promise you, you are going to be OK."

I nodded my head "yes" but I could not say a word. I was too emotional to speak. I wrote down what she said in a small notebook I kept in my purse and promised myself never to forget her words. It was that prophecy that kept me going until it was almost time for me to leave Jonathan.

The last week of February rolled around, and I was anxious to move into my new place. All I had was our clothes, my baby's bassinet, and an air mattress. However, I was overjoyed. I was moving the last few items out of our apartment when Jonathan returned home earlier than usual and caught me loading up the car.

"Whose car is this?" he asked. "And what do you think you're doing? Sneaking out?"

I pushed past him and made my way back into the house to get the baby. I said, "Don't worry about what I'm doing. Shouldn't you be worried about Jasmine?"

Jonathan followed me into the house, grabbed my arm, and snatched the car keys from my hand. He stormed to the back of the house, fussing the entire way. I knew exactly where he was headed. From the dining room, I could hear him open and close the dresser drawers, examining the contents or the lack thereof. I heard him snatch open the closet doors and slide hangers from one side of the closet to the next. When he realized that most of my stuff was gone, he gave me a look of pure hatred.

"You think you so slick," he said with his eyes squinting and lips curled in anger. "I got something for you though. Watch."

He was so predictable. I knew exactly what his next move would be. Sure enough, he cut up the clothes that I had left in the closet as decoys. Unsatisfied, he desperately searched for more items to destroy. When his search didn't turn up anything of value, he became even more enraged.

"Jonathan, I have to go. Can I have my keys back, please?" I asked, holding my hand out impatiently.

"What the fuck is wrong with you? You must be crazy if you think you're getting these keys back!"

"Please just give me the keys, Jonathan."

"You ain't going nowhere. You ass is staying right in this house."

He quickly made his way towards the front door, and I

panicked as I saw my freedom slipping through my fingers. I ran towards the front of the house where the keys to his car were lying on the coffee table. I made it just in time to grab them before he realized what I was doing. As soon as I had his car keys in my hands, I ran back towards the back of the house.

I made it as far as the kitchen, when he caught up to me and tried to wrestle the keys out of my balled-up fist. With our son Junior watching and crying, and our baby boy sleeping in his car seat, Jonathan grabbed a chunk of my hair and yanked my head back. I screamed out in pain. He twisted my arm until it was behind my back, but I refused to give up those keys. Either I was leaving in the rental or his car, but I was getting out of there that day. I don't know where I got the strength to hold onto those keys, but I held on for dear life. I wanted out.

When he saw that I was determined to leave, he grew even more furious and began hitting me over and over again. My son continued screaming and crying in the background. I yelled at Jonathan to stop so that our son would not have to see him beating the crap out of me. It was bad enough that my son had already seen the fight between Jasmine and me. Unfortunately, it seemed as if Jonathan's only concern was stopping me from leaving that house

I finally forced my way out of his grip, but he picked up one of his Timberland boots and began hitting me with it as hard as he could. Finally, it dawned on me that maybe I should call the police. I ran to get the house phone, but before I could dial anything, he snatched it from my hand and ripped the cord out of the wall. Then he threw the phone on the kitchen floor, shattering it to pieces.

My next move happened so fast that I don't know how I got out of the back door and up the stairs without him catching up to me. I must have been running off pure adrenaline. Luckily, our upstairs neighbors, a middle-aged couple, had their back door wide open, so I ran inside crying and breathing heavily. I could barely get the words out of my mouth.

"Please, help me! Please, call the police," I managed to say.

The wife reached for the phone, but when Jonathan appeared behind me in their kitchen, the husband stepped in.

"Hold on a minute," he said to his wife. "Now, we don't know what's going on here. I'm sure these guys can work this out by themselves."

His wife put the phone down, and I started crying even harder. My entire body was shaking so badly that I could barely stand.

I tried to explain to them that he was hurting me and that I was afraid to go back downstairs. In between the tears and the pleading, I remembered all the times I had heard him beating his wife. Not once did I call the police or check on her to make sure she was all right.

"Come on, Mary Kaye," Jonathan begged. "I promise I won't hurt you. Just give me my keys, and I'll give you yours. If you don't call the police, I promise I'll give you the keys back."

I had never seen Jonathan this scared before! The look of desperation in his eyes made me feel a sense of control that was completely foreign to me. I knew he was afraid of getting the police involved, so his goal was to get away from the house as quickly as possible. So, when he backed away slowly down the stairs, I walked towards him to hand him his car keys. Our neighbors watched the exchange as I put his keys in his hand and he placed the rental car keys in mine. He didn't even bother going back inside the apartment. Instead, he left out of the back door and walked around the house to the front yard. I listened for his car as he revved the engine and sped off.

I ran back inside, grabbed my boys, and rushed them into the car. I needed to get as far from this house as possible. Nothing was going to ever make me return to this abuse. The further I drove down the highway, the more at ease I began to feel. I was closing a chapter in my life.

While I could not regain the time I had lost from my youth, I was in my early twenties and determined to experience life on a different level. I had a great job, a new apartment, and my new baby had survived a great deal of trauma in his first six months of life. We were all still here, and after eight years of hell, this was our new beginning.

Chapter 25

Rebound

My boys and I moved into our new apartment at the beginning of the month, and like clockwork, my income tax refund came in the mail. I purchased a used stove and fridge, a sectional sofa with sleeper bed, and a dining room set. I reconnected with Sasha, one of my girlfriends from high school, and we quickly bonded over shopping trips to furnish my new place. I must say, it felt good to have a friend who understood what I had recently survived.

Sasha and I had both experienced abusive relationships, and she knew all too well what it was like to live in fear. I could also be honest with her about the years of psychological abuse, manipulation, and brainwashing that I endured in that relationship with Jonathan. Sasha was determined to help me get over the pain of my past, so she committed herself to making sure I dressed to impress and always had some place to party.

"Nothing takes your mind off your ex like looking for your next," she would say.

We hung out every weekend, hopping from party to party. It felt good to wear sexy outfits and drive to New York to hang out at nightclubs like Shadow, Club Carib, or whatever was popping that weekend. However, the old insecurities would flare up inside of me when men would approach me in the nightclubs. I was not used to the dating scene, and I felt like a child playing dress up.

However, after one shot of Hennessy, I always loosened up enough to dance all night and leave with a purse full of phone numbers. In contrast, during the day I lacked all confidence. I would hold my head down and would be afraid to look people in the eye. Years of intimidation had taken its toll on me. I jumped when people got close to me, and I hated that my nerves were so bad that my hands continually shook. It was embarrassing for me to say the least. For the life of me, I couldn't understand why I was so afraid of people. It was a blessing in disguise when I was court ordered to attend counseling after the fight with Jasmine, so I opened up to my therapist, Dr. Richardson, about my fears and insecurities.

After pouring my heart out to Dr. Richardson, she offered some much-needed words of advice.

"You need to find out what you want to do with your life," she said. "You are more resilient than you realize — just figure out what Mary wants."

I would always remind myself of Dr. Richardson's words, and try my best to figure out who I was and what I wanted. It wasn't easy. For far too long I lived within the confines of the relationship with a master manipulator. Jonathan told me where to go, when to speak, what to do, and how to do it. Now that I was free from having to answer to him, I wasn't quite sure what I wanted.

All I knew was that I wanted to let loose and have fun finally! One weekend, Sasha and I decided to just up and go to Virginia Beach. I had never been to the beach as an adult and was excited about finally seeing the ocean up close and personal. On another weekend, we visited some friends in Maryland and partied the entire time. There was never a dull moment around Sasha.

Meanwhile, Jonathan rarely came by to see the boys during this time. In fact, the most he saw them was when he would ask me to drive thirty minutes up the highway to meet him at a gas station to get a twenty-dollar bill. When the summer rolled around, it was uncomfortably hot in my apartment, and I begged Jonathan to help me buy an air conditioner, but he refused.

One day, Sasha showed up at my house unannounced and called me downstairs to help her get something out of the car. To my surprise, it was a brand-new AC unit! I was so happy that it brought me to tears. Other than immediate family, I have never known someone to care for my children and me as much as she did at that moment. I was so grateful for our friendship. It kept me grounded and distracted from the stress of rebuilding my life.

Even though Sasha was a huge support system for me in more ways than one, the reality of paying bills was starting to set in. One night, I found myself using the last container of baby formula without enough money to purchase more. My baby had to take the special formula for preemies, and the one store that sold this particular kind of formula only had the largest container of that type on their shelves — which was way out of my price range.

I called Jonathan from the store's customer service desk and explained the situation to him.

"Get him the regular formula then," he responded.

"The baby's stomach can't handle other types of formula; he needs this one," I explained. "It's designed specifically for premature babies. Can you please come down here and buy it?"

I explained that I was down to the last bit of formula and only had enough for one more bottle. What was I going to do?

"I'm not driving down there, Mary Kaye! You better figure something out," he said.

Jonathan was only forty-five minutes away, and I knew he had the money.

"Could you send it through Western Union or MoneyGram?"

"No, you wanted to leave and be by yourself, right? So figure something out!"

He hung up on me after that.

I asked the store manager if they could find out if other stores in the area carried the smaller, more affordable container of formula. After making a few phone calls, they discovered that they were the only store in the area that carried that brand and would only have more cans when the shipment came in a few days.

Tears of frustration starting streaming down my face. I felt bad that my son Junior had to see his mom crying in public. I wiped my tears just in time to see an old friend from high school walk into the grocery store.

"Wow, hi, Mary Kaye!" said Dawn, waving.

When I responded with a meek hello through damp eyes, she immediately noticed something was wrong.

"What's the matter?" she asked with a worried look in her eyes.

I ran down the situation to her, and how Jonathan refused to help. I told her how my son was a premature baby and needed this special formula. To my complete surprise, Dawn reached into her wallet without hesitation, pulled out some money, and paid for the formula.

She was an angel that night. I hadn't seen Dawn since we were teenagers, and there we were. Living in the same town and shopping in the same store on the same night — just when I needed someone to step in and intervene. I always said that if I saw her again, I would be a blessing to her and tell her how much her kindness meant to me that night.

Meanwhile, I started experiencing major financial setbacks. While I was paying my rent and bills, and my

1997 Nissan Sentra was well-maintained, I had very little money left over to spare. When a new position in the finance department opened up at my job, I decided to take advantage of this window of opportunity.

With no previous experience in finance, I took my chances and interviewed for the position. I was hired almost on the spot. I learned accounts payable and accounts receivable, which proved to be invaluable for the years to come. Things were looking up.

While riding this wave of good fortune, I saw a commercial for a local hip-hop concert. I decided this was the perfect way to celebrate my new position. I purchased two tickets and immediately phoned Sasha to tell her we were going out that night. I was all dressed up and ready to party when Sasha called me and canceled. She just didn't feel up to it. However, I was determined to celebrate, so I went anyway.

I must admit, it felt awkward sitting alone at a show, but I met the owner of the club and after chatting for a few minutes, I ended up in the VIP section. The headliner, a well-known rap artist, entered the VIP area after the show to sign autographs. When it was my turn to take a photo with him, he put his arm around my waist and pulled me closer to his side.

"I think I want your autograph next," Anthony said in his thick New York accent. "Slide your phone number to my manager before you leave."

His approach caught me completely by surprise, and it floored me that he was interested in me. There were plenty of half-dressed, horny groupies throwing themselves at him, but he wanted my phone number? I wrote down my cell number on a napkin and slipped it to his manager on the low. Shortly after signing autographs and taking pictures, Anthony and his entourage left out of the back of the club. I thought to myself, *I doubt if he'll ever call me.*

Less than an hour later, my phone rang.

"Hey, Beautiful," said a deep, sexy voice on the other line. "You didn't think I would call, did you?" he chuckled.

I played it cool and laughed back.

"Yeah, it is kind of late. What are you guys getting into?"

"We're actually back at the hotel right now. I would like to see you again, though. I can send someone to pick you up right now if you want to join us."

My initial reaction was to keep the party going and join them. You only live once, right? But, then I thought about it and wondered if it would be safe for me to go to a hotel room full of strangers. Plus, he sounded a little tipsy and could only want one thing from me.

"No, thanks," I said. "I need to get some rest and pick up my boys in the morning. You can call me tomorrow though."

"Cool," he said. "Maybe I can take you out for breakfast or lunch then."

When we hung up, my blood rushed. I screamed out loud with excitement. I immediately called Sasha and told her about what just took place. "Girl, you won't believe this!" I said. "He just called and invited me to his room, but I said no. Do you think I did the right thing?"

"I guess we won't know until tomorrow," she said. "But, yes, I think you did the right thing because he was probably testing you."

My excitement continued when Anthony called me the next morning, and we reminisced about the night before.

"There's something about you that just intrigues me. I want to know more about you," Anthony said. "I can tell you've been through a lot, but I can tell you're a strong woman too."

"What else can you see?" I asked.

"I see that you ain't no groupie like some of these other

chicks. You don't sell yourself short, and I can tell you love your kids by the way you talk about them. I respect that."

We talked again later that night after nine o'clock and stayed on the phone until it was almost morning. We laughed, I cried, and we talked about everything from family to our future plans. We found out we had a lot in common. The only problem was that Anthony lived in Georgia, but fortunately, he had another show in New York that next weekend. When he asked if I wanted to join him, I couldn't think of anyplace else I would rather be.

Chapter 26

A Taste of the Glamorous Life

The show was a hip-hop showcase for Vibe Magazine, and there would be lots of celebrities in attendance. I had never dated someone famous before, and this was an exciting new experience for me. One of my major worries was that I would embarrass Anthony and fail to make a good impression on his industry friends. I didn't even know what to wear to an event like this, so Sasha met me at the mall to help me pick out an outfit. She also let me borrow her Maxima so that I wouldn't have to drive to New York in my low-budget vehicle.

Not only was it my first time driving into New York City by myself, but it was also my first official date with Anthony. We had so much fun that night that I wasn't even afraid to ask the other celebrities for their autographs. I told him that I was collecting autographs for my brother so that he wouldn't feel uncomfortable with me acting like a fan.

"If you see anyone you want to kick it with while we're here, just let me know, and I'll slide off to the side," he said.

I was confused. His comment offended me, but I didn't flinch. In the short time that we had known each other, I had already caught on to the fact that he was insecure and jealous. However, I thought I should give him a chance because maybe it was the five glasses of wine that was causing him to become paranoid.

"I don't want to be with anyone other than the man I came here with," I reassured him.

After the showcase, I went to City Island for dinner with Anthony and his friends. He ordered a platter of cookies for me to take home to my sons.

"Always bring them something home," he said with a wink. "That way they'll look forward to you going out on the weekends because they know you'll always bring them something back."

After Anthony walked me to my car, we shared our first kiss. I called him as soon as I drove off, and we talked almost the entire way home. I asked him when he would be in town again, and he told me how he had to fly out of the country to do a show. However, he promised he would make a trip to New York just to see me when he returned. I was in heaven.

There wasn't a day that went by that we did not talk on the phone. We opened up to each other and connected on so many levels. I confided in him about my abusive relationship with Jonathan, and how I had been with him since I was a teenager. I also opened up about my baby and his medical condition, and how he would need brain surgery soon.

He sympathized with my circumstances and assured me that my life was about to change for the better. He said he would always be there for me, no matter what. As promised, when he returned from his overseas tour, he came back to see me. I wasn't used to a man keeping his word. It was like a breath of fresh air.

He took me to meet his parents, and I ended up spending the night at their home. His mom and I quickly bonded, and the next day I met his son from his previous relationship. The following day he stayed overnight at my house. The boys had never seen me with a man other than their dad, so I took them to my sister's house for the night while Anthony and I spent some quality time together. After settling in, we went out to make a run to the grocery store. I wanted to cook for him for a change. While in one of the grocery aisles, one of the store clerks recognized him.

"Are you…?" the clerk asked.

Before Anthony could get a full sentence out, the clerk almost jumped out of his skin.

"Oh my God! I can't believe it's you! Can I get your autograph? I'm such a huge fan!"

I watched in amazement as other people overheard the commotion and started recognizing who he was. It caught me off guard, but at that very moment, I realized that my life could change dramatically. Dating a celebrity was an entirely new way of life. I had to get used to it fast.

I left the supermarket with an entirely different outlook on what our relationship would be like as we spent more time together in public. I could tell Anthony wanted to take things to the next level, and we still hadn't had sex yet. I strongly sensed that he was expecting to move in that direction that very night. After eating, we settled down to watch a movie. Soon, we were kissing, and things started to heat up rapidly.

"I think I'm in love with you, baby girl," Anthony said.

Ummm. I wondered if I had heard him correctly. Was it just me, or did this man who could probably have any woman he wanted tell me that he was in love with me? I couldn't believe what I was hearing! I wasn't sure if he understood the magnitude of what he just said. We'd only known each other for about a month, and we'd only had two dates. Yes, we spent a lot of time on the phone, but love? Did I love him back? Did he mean he was in love with me, or did he just *love* me?

After a few moments of silence, he asked me if I had heard what he said. He was staring at me intently. I still didn't know what to say.

"I just told you I love you, and you don't have anything to say back?" He looked puzzled and annoyed all at the same time.

"I just don't want to be hurt," I said quietly.

He pulled my chin up towards his face and kissed me softly on the nose. "You don't have to say it back," he said. "You don't have to do anything for it. But, I want you to know that I do love you, and I'm going to make sure you and your boys are straight."

I still wasn't ready to have sex with Anthony, and he respected my decision. I worried that our lack of sexual intimacy would chase him off, but that only made him want me more. From that day forward, Anthony treated me like a queen. He sent money when he couldn't be around, he got my car fixed when it broke down, and he even had clothes custom made for me. He flew me across the country to see his concerts, and we dined at the finest restaurants. He spared no expense.

When I mentioned that the prominent radio host Wendy Williams was throwing a major party scheduled the next month, he personally went to radio station 98.7 KISS FM and purchased tickets directly from her. I tuned into Wendy's show faithfully during work hours, and while I was sitting in my office listening to the show, Wendy announced that Anthony was in the building. The studio crew went crazy, and I beamed with excitement as I listened to my man talk to her live on the air about how he made sure to stop by because his lady wanted two tickets to her event.

I was overwhelmed with excitement. I needed to find something special to wear, so I called on my faithful fashionista Sasha. For one reason or another, she had something else going on that night and could not help me find the perfect dress. However, nothing could rain on this parade, so I did the best I could and picked out a jacket to wear with a little black dress.

Things got even more exciting when Anthony sent a stretch limo to pick me up from my house the night of the big event. We arrived at the party with flashing lights immediately capturing our every move on the red carpet. After working our way through a sea of celebs, stopping every few minutes to make introductions, chat, and snap photos, I was escorted to a booth where I sat next to the one and only Mary J. Blige and her then-husband Kendu Isaacs!

Wendy Williams sat on the other side of Kendu alongside her sister. While waiting for Anthony to finish mingling with the crowd, Mary J. and I struck up a conversation. We chatted as if we had known each other for years. The VIP section was buzzing with industry newbies and veterans like Trey Songz, Bobby Brown, Terrence Howard, and many others.

Anthony booked a hotel room for us after the event, and the limo dropped us off at a Hilton not far from where I lived. I knew long before we arrived that tonight was going to be the night we finally made love. It would be the first time being intimate with someone since Jonathan, and I felt nervous and excited all at the same time.

I felt like I was experiencing true love for the first time. Not that teenage love, or the fear that dominated my last relationship, but pure intimacy and closeness that could not be easily broken. After our night together, I had butterflies in my stomach almost every day, and I yearned to have him near me all the time. Our daily conversations intensified, and his parents and I grew closer as time went on. There were times when I would visit them even if Anthony wasn't in town.

When Christmas rolled around, he asked me what my boys wanted as gifts. When I rattled off a list of items, I noticed he was jotting everything down. A few days before Christmas, two huge boxes arrived at my doorstep. Everything my children wanted and more were in those boxes along with some gifts for me as well.

My family was longtime fans of Anthony, so they automatically liked him. My mother was so excited about our relationship and proud to share with friends and family that her daughter was dating a celebrity. It seemed everyone was rooting for us. Things couldn't have been better, or so I thought.

Chapter 27

I Don't Think This Is Going To Work

"What do you think about getting married and moving down to Georgia with me?" Anthony asked.

His question caught me completely off guard.

"What about the kids?" I asked. "I can't just uproot them like that."

"The area I live in has a really good school system," he said. "I checked it out already. And if you're worried about little man and his surgery, there's an excellent hospital too. Come stay for a week or so, and check out the neighborhood and the schools for yourself. Then make a decision. Either way, I'm cool with whatever you decide."

Anthony respected that I did not want to make a hasty decision, but he was also anxious for me to get down there. However, I was appreciative that he didn't make me feel rushed, and I loved the fact that the topic of marriage could come up so easily, as if we had been planning on tying the knot for years.

Anthony booked a flight for me, and when I arrived, I quickly realized that his home was not suitable for children. He had housekeepers that kept everything extra clean, and while my boys were not destructive and disorderly, they were definitely not the quietest when they played around the house. Everything was glass and marble and looked super expensive. I pictured my son throwing a ball in the living room and knocking his Grammy Award off the mantle.

I imagined them running through the house and getting injured on sharp corners and breaking the glass coffee table. I also imagined my little one rolling around in his walker, spilling crumbs wherever he went. It didn't help that Anthony had OCD. He continually checked for dust on countertops and tables and almost threw a fit when I left fingerprints on his kitchen table.

I told him I would consider moving in, but he had to give me some time to figure things out fully. A few months came and went and by mid-March, I made up my mind to move in with Anthony that summer. It gave Junior enough time to finish the school year, and my baby would have his brain surgery by then as well.

Anthony flew me back down to Georgia so that I could become more acquainted with the area. This time the visit was not as pleasant as the last one. On my first night, he decided to take me to a hibachi grill. Spring had arrived, but it was still a little cold out, so I decided to wear my new Coach snow boots to dinner.

"Don't you realize it's spring?" he asked with a look of disgust.

I didn't realize he was so passionate about fashion. I wanted to roll my eyes and say something sarcastic, but I didn't want to ruin the night. "Yes, but it's still cold outside. Plus, these are cute. You don't like them?"

"Whatever," he said, shaking his head.

He held the door for me as we were leaving the house, and before I knew it, I heard a loud thud. I looked back, and he was on the ground struggling to get back on his feet. It turns out that he had slipped on some ice and busted his behind on the concrete. I had to stifle a laugh. So much for it being spring. Instead of laughing in his face, I helped him and tried to appear nonchalant about his slip and fall. There was a lot of tension during dinner that night.

When we got back to the house, he immediately popped open a large bottle of red wine. He turned on some 70s music and drank until he finished the entire bottle. I waited for him to come to bed, and when he finally came into the room, he was so drunk that all he could do was slide under the blanket and fall asleep.

The next day, instead of things getting better, there was an uncomfortable awkwardness between us. He drank another bottle of red wine before dinner that night and was suddenly in the mood to talk.

"I don't think you understand me," he said.

"What do you mean?"

"I mean, every time I open up to you, it's like *crickets*! Dead silence on your end," he said. "What do I need to do to get a reaction out of you? It's like you don't show any emotion. I wonder if you even want to be with a dude like me."

"I don't understand what you're saying, though," I said. "We talk all the time. You know how I feel about you."

"It's like that time I told you I made a record with Snoop Dogg," he explained. "You never even asked to hear it. And when I played it for you, you didn't even say anything! Do you even listen to my music?"

"Yes, I've been listening to your music since I was a little girl. I even have a t-shirt with one of your album covers on it. Come on; you already know that!"

No matter what I said, nothing seemed to get through to him. He was drunk before we finished dinner. When he slumped off into one of the spare bedrooms to listen to more 70s music, I could tell he was hurt and rejected, but I didn't know how to make it up to him. When I checked on him later that night, I planned to butter him up and tell him that I wanted him to come back up north to spend some time with the boys. When I ran the idea by him, his response surprised me.

"I was thinking the same thing," he said. "I would love to spend more time with the boys, especially little man. I can see him growing up calling me daddy; that would be some cool stuff right there."

For a while, things were somewhat back to normal, but we slowly became more and more distant from each other. He would insult me in front of his friends, threaten to leave me behind at his performances if another artist showed interest in me, and his drinking gradually got worse. As the summer drew closer, I started having second thoughts about the relationship. When he attempted to bond with my youngest son, he didn't seem to warm up to him. He would even squirm out of Anthony's arms if he tried to pick him up. I wasn't sure if this was a sign from heaven or not.

Anthony had another show that month at Radio City Music Hall in New York City. I thought this would be the perfect time to see if there was anything left of our relationship. When the evening of the show rolled around, I drove into the city to meet up with him and his brother at a local pizza shop for a quick bite to eat. When I arrived in jeans, a tank top, and a pair of heels, he gave me a look of disapproval.

"Don't worry. I have a change of clothes in the trunk of the car," I reassured him.

I was tired of how he openly displayed his disgust with my clothes. Annoyed, I just went with the flow and forced a smile.

"With you, you never know," Anthony said. "I mean, last time you showed up in a winter outfit in the spring. Now that was dumb funny!"

He and his brother burst into laughter at my expense.

"Yeah, tell that to the ice you slipped on," I muttered under my breath.

I didn't want to get into it with him in front of his brother, so I just ignored him and enjoyed my slice of pizza. Shortly after, we went backstage in preparation for show time. While waiting in the green room with rap legends like Nas, DJ Jazzy Jeff, Talib Kweli, and Common, I watched as they all joked around and swapped memories of coming up during the golden age of hip-hop.

The night was perfect for Anthony. Regardless of the growing wedge between us, I was happy for him. It was a major event that helped to relaunch his media presence. However, something still didn't feel quite right as far as I was concerned. The first thing that rubbed me the wrong way was that he ignored me half the night. I watched the other artists with their girlfriends, and I saw that there was a level of trust that existed among them that Anthony and I just did not have.

While the wives and girlfriends were free to mingle with the room, Anthony kept his eye on me all night and would get upset if I held the slightest conversation with any other celebrity. By the end of the night, he was drunk and filled with jealousy. When Talib Kweli tried to introduce me to his daughter who he had brought to the show that night, he interrupted the conversation and told me he was ready to leave. I was embarrassed by his insecurity.

"I guess you're ready to go back home?" he said.

"Huh?" I said, puzzled.

"You want to go back home or what?"

"I'm cool," I responded. "I'm with you."

For some reason, I felt very small and insignificant with Anthony. It felt like I was just a placeholder at his events, and he controlled my every move without me even realizing it. I also felt uneasy because it dawned on me that maybe this relationship was not going to work. Perhaps I wasn't ready for a rebound relationship after all that Jonathan had put me through. Maybe this was not my dream man after all. I fought back the tears as we entered an elevator with Erykah Badu and Common. How embarrassing!

We went back to the hotel, and before we could settle in, his brother came and joined us. Having his brother there angered me even further because I had hoped Anthony and I could finally talk things over. Didn't he realize that we needed some quality time together so we could talk about his jealous ways? He needed to know how he was making me feel, and how embarrassing it was to be in public with him at times.

His brother left after an hour or so, and we finally got a chance to talk.

"I don't think this is going to work," I blurted out.

Before I could say anything else, tears started to flow. I didn't know what else to say. All I knew was that I felt trapped. I didn't want to stay in a relationship because of money and fame. I was tired of the concerts, the groupies, the drinking, and most of all, the jealousy. I was tired of feeling like I had no voice.

I had spent far too much of my life with men who stifled my opinions and kept me in fear. I wondered why I kept attracting older men that desired to dominate me. It was as if they all wanted to destroy something innocent and beautiful. I finally decided to take ownership of my life and move on.

The relationship abruptly came to an end that very night. We held each other as we slept fully dressed, and when we woke up the next day, we moved around in complete silence as we showered, dressed, and gathered our things. The only words we said to each other was "goodbye" as I left the hotel room with my duffle bag in hand and my heart broken. I got into my car and drove home.

Chapter 28

I Want It All

Although the breakup with Anthony hurt, I felt liberated. For the first time in years, I felt independent and free. The drive home after leaving that hotel room was one of the longest drives ever, but it gave me time to reflect on what I wanted out of life. I had quit my job in preparation for the move to Georgia, so I was an unemployed, single mother of two. I struggled, but I was free. I cried many nights, but some of those tears were tears of release. It was bottled up pain that could finally flow.

I thought I would break and call Anthony just to talk about what went wrong, and if there was any way we could fix it. To my pleasant surprise, I rejected his calls and resisted the urge to reach out to him. Admittedly, I was broken and confused, but I was finally free.

While I would like to say I remained free, the truth is I returned to what was familiar after only a short period of singleness. Since the age of thirteen, I had always had a companion. I always had the attention of the opposite sex, and it didn't take long for me to start craving that attention all over again.

Not to mention I had become familiar with a lavish lifestyle I could no longer afford. Suddenly, I wanted money, nice clothes, and expensive cars. I went into a state of depression and returned to a bad habit that I thought I had gotten over. I started taking what I wanted to make myself feel better.

As my closet filled up with clothes and my shoes piled up from floor to ceiling from my shoplifting sprees, I started to feel better. Every weekend I would get more stuff to fill the void I was experiencing, and finally, I had more clothes than I could have ever imagined. However, there was another void that desperately needed to be filled.

I developed an unhealthy desire to use men to get what I wanted as a means to make them pay for all the years of abuse, manipulation, cheating, and lies. I wanted to hurt them, but I didn't realize I was going to hurt myself the most in the process.

While pumping my gas one day, a cute middle-aged man pulled up at the pump opposite to me. I admired the BMW he was driving, the stylish sunglasses, and the expensive looking watch on his wrist. Now, if I could just peep his shoe game, that would be the icing on the cake.

"Hey, sexy," he said. He bit his lip as if he wanted to taste me right then and there.

His voice was saturated in a heavy New York accent that reminded me of Anthony, and I could smell his cologne from where I was standing. The song "Glamorous" by Fergie was spilling through his open windows. I was impressed with his style.

"Hello," I said with a flirtatious smile. "Nice car."

"Thanks, love. You want one?"

"Who wouldn't?"

He chuckled. "Take my number, sweetie. My name is Esteban. What's yours?"

We hit it off immediately and didn't waste any time. For our first date, he surprised me with a spa package in the city followed by dinner at a French restaurant. He took me on shopping sprees and bought me expensive clothes at Saks and Nordstrom.

During one shopping trip, in particular, the young lady at the register was amazed at all the things Esteban was buying for me. "Wow, you have like seven pairs of True Religion jeans up here," she said. "Can I get one?"

"Slow your roll, sweetie," said Esteban. "You're gonna have to work for that."

He gave the cashier a wink as she bagged up the items.

"Give shorty your number, Mary. Maybe you can school her on some things."

At that exact moment, I suspected I had bitten off more than I could chew with Esteban. When we left the store and drove down the highway back towards my house, he got off an exit, drove to a secluded area, and told me to get out of the car.

Confused, I looked around and asked him where we were.

"Don't worry, sweetie, you just worry about paying me back for all these clothes I just bought for your sexy ass."

I guess I still looked confused, because he grabbed me by the chin and tilted my face up towards his.

"Oh, you thought all that shit was free? Turn your ass around."

While I wanted to have sex with Esteban eventually, this was not how I had envisioned our first encounter. I was sure I could stand up to him, so I looked him square in the eyes and said, "No."

"Bitch, do you want me to leave you out here in the middle of fucking nowhere?" he said. "Now, turn around and pull your motherfucking skirt up!"

My nerves started to kick in. I was determined not to let him see how scared I was, so I just turned around and pulled up my skirt, telling myself that it was OK because I planned on giving him some anyway. Esteban snatched at my underwear and pulled them down until they were around my knees. I could hear him hurriedly unbuckling his belt and unzipping his pants.

"Do you have a condom?" I asked nervously.

"Bitch, you trying to tell me I need one or some shit?"

"No, I..."

Before I could finish speaking, he was already inside me. Raw. I couldn't believe what was happening. A voice inside my head told me just to enjoy it. *Pretend you want it, Mary, and you will get through this in no time.* I knew the logic was all wrong, but it was the only thing I could do to keep myself from going crazy. I wanted to fight him off, but I was afraid. Plus, this was nothing new. I had been here before. *Just enjoy it, Mary.*

After he finished, he kissed me gently on the side of my face and spoke softly in my ear. "You are fucking amazing! You know that? I ain't never letting you go, bitch."

I had never seen this side of him before. I felt conned into whatever this was. This was not the Esteban I had met at the gas station not too long ago.

He blasted love songs while we drove to my house in silence, as if we had just come down from a romantic evening. I didn't even want the clothes that were in the back seat of the car. When I got home, I went straight to bed, leaving all the clothes in the bags. I told myself that I would return the items for cash and pay bills with the money. I needed to get away from this man quick, fast, and in a hurry. If only it were that simple.

Chapter 29

A Self-Laid Trap

The next day, Esteban called me to apologize. "You just don't realize how sexy you are, sweetie," he said. "You have something special, and I want to teach you how to have these niggas out here eating out the palm of your hand."

He told me I could make a man fall in love on sight, and that I needed to capitalize on my youth. I sensed where he was going with the conversation, so I told him I needed some time alone for a while.

"Esteban, I've been through a lot. I need some time to be by myself. I've never really tried that before."

"Don't walk away from me now, sweetie," he begged.

Then, he said the magic words.

"I think I'm falling for you. I don't think I ever felt like this about any other female this fast."

His words reminded me so much of that night with my ex-boyfriend Terrence. Terrence cried and lied right to my face, all while professing his microwaved version of love. Sadly, although the warning signs were all there, I continued my relationship with Esteban. He showered me with gifts as a show of gratitude for sticking by his side. For some reason that I can't fully explain, I desperately wanted to hold on to this man, regardless of how disrespected and used I felt. While it appeared he only wanted me for sex, his guilt trips and his desire to keep me in his life made me feel wanted and needed.

It felt good to have a man declare his love for me once again, even if I suspected it was all a lie. However, when you've been hurt by the truth for so long, you start finding comfort in lies. The fantasy of a man begging for me to take him back felt good and familiar. Although I knew Esteban had a hidden agenda, I enjoyed the attention he gave me. However, somewhere twisted between the fantasies and insecurities of wanting to be loved was pure revenge.

The revenge had more to do with what he and other men had stolen from me. I felt tricked into giving up my body over and over again. Now I wanted something in return as well.

One evening, Esteban and I were talking about our favorite movies, and mine just happened to be "The Mack." I told him how I had a crush on Goldie, the main character.

"Matter of fact, you kind of look like Goldie," I told him.

"Word? That's your favorite movie, for real?" he said with a surprised tone in his voice. He was impressed that someone so prissy like me would be into a movie about pimping.

"You ever heard of a book called 'Pimp' by Iceberg Slim?" I asked.

"Of course. Come on, look who you are talking to, sweetie."

"Well, my last boyfriend got me addicted to that book and introduced me to 'The Mack.' Ever since then, I've been fascinated with the pimp game."

I waited intently for his response, because my goal was to impress him with my knowledge about the pimp game somehow. I could almost hear the wheels turning in his brain, but I was determined only to give him a tease. However, what started out as a tease turned into a self-laid trap.

If I had known what would happen next, I would have never opened this dangerous door. Esteban took our conversation to the next level and concocted a full-blown plan for us. I was completely caught off guard when he showed up the next day with a new cellphone he'd purchased for me. We were sitting on the couch in a hotel room, drunk and high on weed.

"I need you to carry this phone with you at all times," he said in between puffs of smoke. "I should always be able to reach you. That's rule number one." He warned me not to use the phone for anything other than to contact him.

"Remember how I told you to capitalize on your youth?" he reminded me. "Well, you can make a whole lot of money in these here streets, but I need you to trust me. That's rule number two. Trust me, sweetie. These broads out here sleeping with cats and don't have nothing to show for it! You know a little bit about the pimp game, right?" He winked at me and waited for my response.

I nodded my head "yes." However, I was still naively unsure about where this conversation was headed.

"Well, all you need is a couple of these rich, white motherfuckers to fall for your sexy ass, and you set for life. Don't worry, bitch; I'm going to always be here for you. You ain't got to worry about that," he said. "You can tell them white men I'm your uncle or some shit; I don't care. But we can both get rich off of that good shit you got between your legs."

It was then that I figured out what Esteban was proposing. I suppose I wasn't giving him the response he was looking for, because he quickly became more direct and blunt with his proposition.

"Look here, bitch. I need you to listen to me and listen to me real good," he said with slight irritation in his voice. "We can make a whole lot of money if you work this here thing right. We can have a whole stable of bitches, you hear me? You can be my bottom hoe and get all them chicks in line!"

By now, he was so animated that his words were slurring badly, and spit was flying from his mouth. He was drunk.

I heard everything Esteban said, but I felt a mixture of amusement, shock, disbelief, fear, and confusion. I didn't know what to think or feel! Clearly, he was drunk and excited, but this man had a plan and was not taking no for an answer. It felt like I was losing control of my mind all over again. I remember feeling like I did not have a say so in my life, just like I used to feel with Jonathan.

There was a strong urge to do as I was being told — to listen to this man because somehow he was going to provide everything my heart desired. Love. Acceptance. Money. Support. Excitement. Power.

However, I was still broken. Therefore, manipulation came easy. Control of my mind seemed to be effortless on his part. When Esteban confessed that he had run into some financial troubles, my heart began to soften. When he told me that he wanted to give me things I've never had and take me places I've never been, my heart softened some more. He even told me how he could barely afford the maintenance on his BMW, and how he was struggling from check to check.

"The reason I keep booking these rooms for us is that I'm ashamed of my studio apartment," he confessed. "I couldn't let you see me living like that. Things are mad tight, ma. We can have everything we want and then some if we do this thing right. I want you pushing your own BMW by the end of the year."

Esteban took me by the chin and pushed my head up so I could look at him. He was crying. Oh, here we go again! Do men think that's the way to my heart or something? The tears got me every time.

"I got you," I said reassuringly in my sexiest voice. "What you need me to do to make this happen, Daddy?"

I was in full vixen mode at this point. It was as if someone had downloaded an entirely different personality into my system. Esteban's whole demeanor changed as well. He literally jumped up and started pacing the room — all the while giving me step-by-step instructions about how he wouldn't have me on the streets, but at corporate parties and events.

"These white motherfuckers ain't gon' know what hit 'em!" he said with excitement.

"Why don't you send me out to the strip clubs?" I suggested.

"Nah, I don't want you stripping. That's not you, ma."

"No, not to strip, daddy. I'm talking about going to the clubs to get customers."

"You a fucking genius, bitch! That's why I love you; you know that? And another thing; call them clients, not customers. You want everything to be professional."

The next day, we went shopping for some new clothes. He wanted me to wear the most seductive, alluring outfits we could find. He gave me three additional rules: no alcohol, no black clubs, and no black men. I would only go to strip clubs out of town to lessen the chances of running into anyone I knew.

Our first stop was about two hours from my house. While Esteban settled in at the bar, I inquired about auditioning for a job as a dancer. While watching a couple of girls on stage, I chatted with a few customers until I got enough courage to go in for the kill.

My first john paid me one hundred dollars just to give him oral sex in his car a few blocks away from the club. I admit this was a low amount, but Esteban never told me what to charge these men. Before the night was over, I had sex with two other "clients" and my first night's pay totaled seven hundred dollars.

Although I felt a rush of excitement at the end of the night, I still felt cheap. I felt even cheaper as I watched Esteban count my money in the hotel room that night with a silly grin on his face. He laughed and danced around the room, in celebration of "our" first night on the job.

"Imagine what we're going to have by this weekend?" he said.

It was only Thursday. I had to get up and go to work at my nine to five the next morning and do this all over again tomorrow night. The adrenaline would keep me going, I supposed.

The next day I bought a few Red Bull drinks to keep me awake. I had one to get me through the day and one later that evening before we went to a new strip club. When we arrived, I was immediately intimidated by all the beautiful women in the room.

The first club was sleazy, but this was upscale. The women looked like models, and the men seemed preoccupied with getting private dances. I had to step my game up. I went to the bar and asked to speak with the club manager. When the bartender asked my reason for wanting a manager, I asked him if they needed extra girls.

"Do you think they'll let me audition tonight?" I asked. I made sure to put on the most flirtatious smile I could manage through my nervousness.

"Follow me," he said. "I think you'll fit right in."

Esteban's watchful eyes followed us as the bartender took me to the back of the club to the manager's office. The manager motioned for me to come inside, and the bartender went back to his post. He gave me a wink and a thumbs-up before closing the office door behind him.

The manager, who still hadn't said anything, intently looked over some paperwork, signing his name every few pages, while another employee stared at a few television monitors that displayed the club's activities from different angles. Finally, the manager turned his full attention toward me. He pulled off his glasses, leaned forward, and looked at every part of my body except my face.

"Can you dance?" he asked.

"Of course," I said.

"You ready to dance tonight?"

"Absolutely."

"OK, here's the thing. No full nudity, just topless," he explained. "You audition, and whatever money you make on that stage is yours to keep. However, if you do any private dances, we get a cut. Now, before you go out there, I need you to take off your clothes for me." He then turned to the man sitting at the cameras. "Fred, give us a minute."

Fred stood up from the television monitors and walked out, leaving us alone in the office. I started to feel claustrophobic all of a sudden.

Chapter 30

Living My Life On Stages

I must have looked confused because the club manager repeated himself. "Take off your clothes, hun. Come on, don't tell me you're nervous! If you can't take your clothes off in here, how are you going to do it out there?"

"It's not that," I said. "I was just caught off guard, that's all."

I pulled my top over my head and slid down my jean miniskirt. Kicking the skirt off to the side, I reached behind my back and unbuttoned my lacy pink and black bra. The manager never took his eyes off me, nor did I take my eyes off him.

"Turn around," he said.

I turned, my back now facing him. I shuttered when I felt his cold hands slowly glide over my hips and butt as if he was analyzing the shape of my body. Suddenly, he spread my butt cheeks open and kneeled down on the floor. I panicked and turned around in anger.

"What are you doing?!" I demanded.

"Lower your voice and be cool," he said calmly. "I'm just making sure you're the right fit for us. When you bend over on that stage, everyone is going to see exactly what I see right now. Trust me and just relax," he said. "Now turn back around, hun. Trust me."

I reluctantly turned around again. While I was more prepared to feel his hands on my body, they still felt ice cold, and I jumped at his touch. I shivered as he spread my cheeks open again, but more cautiously this time. He put some oil on his finger and wiped it down the middle of my butt. I grimaced and bit the inside of my lip, praying he would hurry up with his "inspection."

Why his next move did not make me gather my clothes and run out of there screaming, I will never know. He reached under me and groped at my vagina. As if that wasn't enough, he slowly rubbed his wet fingers back and forth between my legs, feeling his way around. I thought he was almost done, but without warning, he suddenly jammed what felt like his entire hand inside of me! I yelled out in pain.

"What the hell is wrong with you!" I yelled, grabbing at his arm and pushing him away from me. "Where are my clothes?"

I looked around for my things, but my tank top and skirt were nowhere in sight. I quickly scanned the room to no avail. That's when he grabbed my arms and pulled me close to his chest.

"Don't think I don't know who you are," he whispered in my ear. "Club Allure sent us your photo and told us all about you and what you're up to."

He released my arms and put his hands on each side of my body as if to warn me that I was under his control now. My body shook with fear and the ice-cold air conditioner in the office.

"No worries," he reassured. "I won't have you arrested for prostitution. Not yet. Just follow my rules, and you can work here with no problem."

I refused to let him see me scared, so I toughened up and looked him square in the eyes. "What do I need to do?" I asked.

He chuckled.

"That's what I'm talking about. First, we need to finish our little interview. So, how much do you charge?"

Although I gave him my price, I fought back the tears as I allowed this total stranger to violate me in his office. The fast life was not the life I envisioned for myself. I was only in my twenties, and it felt like I had been molested, raped, and abused more times than I could count. I just wanted it to be over. I wished I had something stronger than a Red Bull in my system.

When it was over, he allowed me to change into my stage clothes and audition for the customers. I took all my frustration out on that stage. I danced seductively, savagely, and so fiercely that my body was dripping with sweat by the time I was done.

Even Esteban couldn't help but to come to the stage and throw out some of his money. After three short songs, I collected my cash and exited the stage with one of the customers who requested a private dance. Esteban winked at me as we passed each other. My anger wouldn't even allow me to crack a smile.

I became a regular dancer at this club until one night the manager caught me soliciting a customer for some "outside activity." He figured out what was going on when the customer decided to wait for me in the parking lot instead of at the hotel next door like I had asked.

As I made my way to the car, the manager ran outside and asked the customer to please come back in for a drink.

"Hey, the next drink is on the house, dude. Just come back inside. She's bad news, man."

I turned around and gave the manager an angry stare. "Look, we know each other, all right?" I tried explaining. "We're just going to hang out and get something to eat."

The customer went along with my story and refused to come back into the club.

"You're done here; you know that, right?" the manager said, pointing his finger in my face. He shook his head and walked back into the club, while my john and I pulled out of the parking lot.

Although I could probably talk my manager into giving me another chance, I knew I could never go back to that club again. Esteban had stopped coming along after I started dancing, and I always lied to him about how much money I was making.

Each weekend he would come to collect *our* money. As the money became less and less, he became agitated and violent. I told myself that he was just playing the game and that he thought he had to smack me around so he could keep pretending to be a real pimp.

"You owe me more money, bitch! I taught you this game," Esteban would say. "I bought you that phone, the clothes you got on, the shoes you wear. I put food in your kids' mouths, hoe! You violatin'!"

One day he slapped me so hard his ring hit the corner of my mouth, and I started bleeding. Seeing the blood didn't seem to slow him down because he grabbed me by the throat and began choking me until I was unconscious.

When I woke up, my clothes were off, and he was having sex with me. How long had I been unconscious? My mouth felt swollen. I could taste blood.

"That's right, bitch, wake the fuck up," he said in between heavy breathing. "Don't think I won't know where to find you if you try to walk out on me, bitch. I'll find you, and I'll slit your motherfucking throat."

He punched me in the face and on the side of my head. I made a feeble attempt at blocking him, but he grabbed my hands and held them together. My crying didn't even seem to bother him.

"You supposed to have two or three bitches working for us by now. What the hell happened to that? You supposed to be my bottom bitch! I swear I feel like snapping your neck right now!"

He pushed himself off me, grabbed me, pulled me off the floor, and banged my head against the wall. I experienced migraines for about a week following this incident. From that day forward, the threats were non-stop, and I was in constant fear for my life. I wanted to get away from him, but it felt nearly impossible. I knew the only real way that I could dodge him was to change my routine, my address, and my phone number.

The first part of my plan was to switch clubs without letting him know where I was working. He stopped following me around every night a long time ago, and I was pretty much fending for myself every weekend. I lied and told him that I had problems getting childcare for my son because my cousin was now working an overnight shift. This explained the decrease in money I was making. I also let the battery die on the phone he had bought for me and told him the phone was broken. All the while, I continued stripping and prostituting on the weekends, slowly saving up enough money to move out of my apartment and into a better neighborhood.

Soon, I had all the money I needed. One day he dialed my regular cellphone from a strange number, and I unknowingly accepted his call.

"Where you been at, ma?" he said in a soft, concerned voice. "I've been missing you like crazy. I need to see you."

"Whose phone are you using?" I asked. "Anyway, I have my boys with me, so I can't see you right now." I never allowed Esteban around my children before, so I knew I could keep him away when they were with me.

"When can I see you then?"

"I don't know. Things have been kind of hectic without a babysitter."

"How you making ends meet, though? I know you gotta take care of your two-piece," he said, referring to my kids.

"Actually, I was able to catch a break," I explained. "I had a car accident about a year ago, and I just got the settlement money."

I regretted the words coming out of my mouth as quickly as I had spoken them.

"Oh word?" he said, chuckling.

I didn't see anything funny, but OK.

"Yo, I'm glad you told me that, ma. You have always been honest with me. That's why I like you."

He placed me on hold as he chatted with someone in the background. It sounded like a female giggling, but I forced myself to hold back my questions because I planned to end this relationship anyway. He didn't know I was moving out of my apartment, and soon I would be free from him once and for all.

"Ma, I'm gonna need that money."

"What? What money?"

"That settlement money you just told me about."

I snickered into the phone. "Yeah, OK," I muttered under my breath.

"Listen to me, and listen to me well, ma. I'm about to put you on to this rich motherfucker I met out here in the Hamptons, and that little bit of change you got ain't gonna be nothing compared to what you about to have. I just need you to take the train down here and come see your daddy, OK? Do you hear me?"

He was rambling fast and slick, and I finally saw straight through all his pimp talk. Through all the lies about us picking out matching 745s and living in a dream house while we travel the world, I finally saw that he was just using me. Plain and simple.

"Hello? You still there?" I could hear the excitement in Esteban's voice. I could always tell when he was running game. I just got caught up in it for a little while, but I had finally reached my breaking point.

"Yeah, I'm here, but I can't give you that money." Click.

After hanging up the phone, I feared that I had just started something I could not finish. He called back twice and gave up after a few text messages. Would he try to come out here unannounced? Was my life in danger? Were my kids safe?

I went to my sister's house, and we spent the night there for a few days. I told her that my apartment wasn't ready and that I needed to stay until it was time to move in. Surprisingly, Esteban never called again. It helped that he lived in another state, but he was still close enough that I was always looking over my shoulder.

Chapter 31

From Rejection to Redemption

In the days that followed, I found myself single, insecure, and unsettled. I didn't trust men, so I focused on dancing in the club and using guys for money. I dated a few of my customers for weeks at a time until I got bored and moved on. There was the Porsche-driving, Italian business owner. Then it was the Greek living on his family's estate in Greenwich, Connecticut. Then there was the young Russian architect who caught me cheating on him with one of my "clients."

I wanted to feel liberated, but instead, familiar feelings of rejection haunted me for months, even years later. Only this time, the rejection wasn't coming from men, but from deep within my subconscious mind. As negative thoughts began to flood my soul, I reflected on the many mistakes I stumbled over throughout my life. I thought about all the things I said and all the things I did that I wished to God I could take back.

I felt like a complete failure. I felt like everyone was watching me with large, critical eyes, wondering why I would make such poor decisions, when I was going to step out of this downward spiral, and when I would wake up and realize the potential that was inside of me all along!

My mind went back to when I was just a little girl pretending to be something I wasn't. Pretending to be sexually promiscuous long before that became my reality. I ended up creating a reputation for myself based on the lies I told myself and others. Why was I so bent on destroying what little innocence I had back then? The only plausible explanation I could conjure up was that I blinded myself by a need for acceptance. I tainted my thinking by the images I saw on television — the rap and R&B videos showing me that to gain attention you had to dress seductively. You had to be sensual and sexually free like some of the female rap artists of the 90s, not timid and tomboyish like me. I simply believed I was not good enough.

My self-image was stained. I was so cruel to myself, and I taught others to degrade me as well. In the meantime, many took advantage of my vulnerability. I had no idea that I deserved better. I told myself that I would speak the truth of what I had endured all these years and be free from shame and guilt. Through all the heartbreaks, all the relationships, and all the disappointments, I felt like I had seen enough pain to last ten lifetimes.

When I reflected on my mistakes, my faults, and my failures, I thought about the many times I felt ashamed of myself — too ashamed to even look in the mirror. Now, I was alone with myself, and I forced myself to look inside my heart and face the layers of lies, the mountains of mistakes, and the deep-rooted destruction that tried to kill me so many times before. What I saw almost broke me, but when I recovered, I rediscovered myself. I learned that I always loved me. I just never learned how to show myself how much I truly loved Mary!

Something awakened in me and stood up in my very soul. I suddenly realized there was nothing more important at that moment than to look deep down inside of myself and bring Mary to the forefront. I had to stop crumbling under the mistakes and missteps. I had to stop cowering from abuse and manipulation. I had to stop carrying the weight of self-loathing and low self-esteem.

I came out of hiding.

In Closing...

Dear Readers,

"Stripped" could not possibly contain all that I endured throughout these difficult years. I chose to deal with the various relationships and encounters that nearly tore me apart because they provide a clear picture of who I am and what led to the destructive choices I made in life. I was stripped. Hiding behind years of sexual abuse was a little girl who has now grown into a beautiful woman but still afraid of her past.

Now, the word "stripped" takes on a new meaning. Stripped now represents stripping away the lies, rejection, pain, and low self-esteem. Redemption came the moment I conjured up the courage to start writing this book and uncovering the ugly secrets I had held onto for so long. It feels good to be free!

After all the pain and trauma, I am a wife, mother, second-year law student at New York Law School, a #1 International Best-Selling Author, recipient of a Doctorate of Philosophy from CICA International University, and award-winning founder of two non-profit organizations, Blue Wing and a Prayer and Triumph Community Outreach. Even with all this, I know that there is even more for me ahead. If I can bounce back and become all that God has destined for me to be, so can you!

Meanwhile, I have a part II in the works, which deals with my life after my "awakening." Look out for "The Comeback Queen: From Trauma to Triumph" projected to be released by 2019. Also, check out my #1 Best-Seller, "The Art of Unlearning" now available at www.amazon.com.

Visit www.comebackqueen.org to find out more about me, my non-profit organizations, and how we help prevent suicide, promote prosperity, and motivate others to find momentum towards redemption in life.

Please continue to the next page where I have included various national resources that may be of assistance to those in abusive relationships, have thoughts of suicide, battle depression, struggle with substance abuse, or need general social services.

Resources

Please visit The American Foundation for Suicide Prevention at https://afsp.org/find-support/resources/ for available nationwide resources that can assist with anxiety, sexual abuse, mental health disorders, depression, substance abuse, and more.

Meanwhile, if you or someone you know have thoughts of suicide or have attempted suicide, please visit, call, or text:

24/7 Crisis Hotline: National Suicide Prevention Lifeline Network
http://www.suicidepreventionlifeline.org/
1-800-273-TALK (8255)

Crisis Text Line
Text TALK to 741-741 to text with a trained crisis counselor from the Crisis Text Line for free, 24/7

Have you or someone you know experienced sexual abuse?

RAINN National Sexual Assault Hotline
1-800-656-HOPE (4673)

National Teen Dating Abuse Helpline
1-866-331-9474

If you took away learning from this book or found it helpful, I'd be very grateful if you'd post a short review on Amazon. Your support does make a difference, and I read all the reviews personally so I can get your feedback and make this book even better.

If you'd like to leave a review, then all you need to do is type in "Stripped: A Journey From Rejection to Redemption on Amazon" in the search bar of your internet browser, and the link will show up. Click on the link to leave your review.

Thanks again for your support!

Made in the USA
Columbia, SC
19 March 2018